Envision It! Handbook

Reading STREET
Grade 6

PEARSON

Glenview, Illinois
Boston, Massachusetts
Chandler, Arizona
Upper Saddle River, New Jersey

ISBN-13: 978-0-328-58089-7
ISBN-10:   0-328-58089-9
1 2 3 4 5 6 7 8 9 10 V042 18 17 16 15 14 13 12 11 10 09

Envision It! Handbook

Contents

Let's Think About Strategies......................4

Comprehension Strategies
and Anchor It!...5–25

    Background Knowledge 6
    Important Ideas.......................................8
    Inferring 10
    Monitor and Clarify 12
    Predict and Set Purpose............................14
    Questioning 16
    Story Structure 18
    Summarize 20
    Text Structure 22
    Visualize 24

Let's Think About Skills 26

Comprehension Skills,
    See It! Say It! Do It!, and Lessons 27–111
    Author's Purpose 28
    Cause and Effect....................................36
    Compare and Contrast.............................44
    Draw Conclusions..................................52

Comprehension Skills (continued)

Fact and Opinion 60

Generalize 68

Graphic Sources.................................... 76

Literary Elements 86

Main Idea and Details 96

Sequence 104

Let's Think About Vocabulary............... 112

Words! and Vocabulary Lessons...................113–187

Related Words 114

Context Clues....................................... 115

Antonyms and Synonyms 128

Prefixes and Suffixes 142

Dictionary and Thesaurus 156

Multiple-Meaning Words........................ 164

Base Words/Root Words/
Word Origins 176

Let's Think About Genre 188

Genre Charts 189

Let's Think About...

Comprehension Strategies

Comprehension strategies are ways to think about reading in order to better understand what you read.

As you read,
- focus on the text.
- try to make sense of what you are reading.
- notice when you don't understand something.
- figure out how to understand confusing parts.

Ready to Try It?

Envision It! Visual Strategies

Background Knowledge

Important Ideas

Inferring

Monitor and Clarify

Predict and Set Purpose

Questioning

Story Structure

Summarize

Text Structure

Visualize

Background Knowledge

Background knowledge is what you already know about a topic based on your reading and personal experience. Make connections to people, places, and things from the real world. Use background knowledge before, during, and after reading.

To use background knowledge
- with fiction, preview the title, author's name, and illustrations
- with nonfiction, preview chapter titles, headings, graphics, and captions
- think about what you already know
- think about your own experiences

Let's Think About Reading!

When I use background knowledge, I ask myself
- Does this character remind me of someone?
- How is this story or text similar to others I have read?
- What else do I already know about this genre or topic?

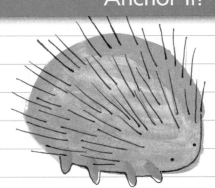

Background Knowledge
Hatchet
by Gary Paulsen

When I use background knowledge, I think about what I know from:

my own life (text-to-self)   the world (text-to-world)

other things I've read (text-to-text)

I made these connections while reading Hatchet.

 I've been to Northern Canada before, and it was cold when I was there, so it's probably cold where Brian is.

 Sometimes certain noises scare me at night. I get how Brian would be scared when he hears a slithering sound!

I've read a book about animals defending themselves, so I know that porcupines release pointy quills when they get scared or attacked.

At first I thought the noise Brian heard might have been a bear or a snake. But when Brian felt the needles in his leg, I knew it was a porcupine.

Important Ideas

Important ideas are essential ideas and supporting details in a nonfiction selection. Important ideas include information and facts that provide clues to the author's purpose.

To identify important ideas
- read all titles, headings, and captions
- look for words in italics, boldface print, or bulleted lists
- look for signal words and phrases: *for example, most important,* and others
- use photographs, illustrations, or other graphic sources
- note how the text is organized—cause and effect, problem and solution, question and answer, or other ways

Let's **Think** About **Reading!**

When I identify important ideas, I ask myself
- What information is included in bold, italics, or some other special lettering?
- What details support important ideas?
- Are there signal words and phrases?
- What do illustrations, photos, diagrams, and charts show?
- How is the text organized?
- Why did the author write this?

Important Ideas
Into the Ice
by Lynn Curlee

I read <u>Into the Ice</u>, and thought about the problems explorers faced while trying to get to the North Pole. Some important ideas were:

• Many people wanted to be first to reach the North Pole.
• In 1896, explorers went further than anyone in recorded history.
• Many explorers didn't make it all the way because they ran out of food and supplies.
• People tried reaching the North Pole by balloon and by dog sled, but weather got in the way both times.
• Researchers say no one actually reached the North Pole back then.
• Joseph Fletcher flew to the North Pole in 1952. He is known as the first person to really stand on the North Pole.

All of this information helps me understand that Polar expeditions were dangerous. Explorers risked their lives trying to reach the North Pole!

Inferring

When we **infer** we use background knowledge with clues in the text to come up with our own ideas about what the author is trying to present.

To infer

- identify what you already know
- combine what you know with text clues to come up with your own ideas

Let's Think About Reading!

When I infer, I ask myself
- What do I already know?
- Which text clues are important?
- What is the author trying to present?

Inferring
Mother Fletcher's Gift
by Walter Dean Myers

FACTS AND DETAILS	INFERENCES
Mother Fletcher was a "legend" on 145th street.	A lot of people must know Mother Fletcher in the neighborhood.
O'Brien says that it's really hard to get a doctor to make house calls in Mother Fletcher's neighborhood.	Maybe the neighborhood isn't considered safe.
Mother Fletcher's apartment is "small but spotless."	Mother Fletcher must be proud of what she has.
Mother Fletcher knits O'Brien a sweater.	She sounds like a very kind and thoughtful person.
O'Brien doesn't give a direct answer to Mother Fletcher's invitation to Christmas dinner.	O'Brien doesn't really want to go, but doesn't want to hurt Mother Fletcher's feelings, either, or be the "bad guy."
Mother Fletcher says, "The more you expect the more you get your heart broke up."	By not expecting the O'Briens to show up for dinner, Mother Fletcher wouldn't be disappointed if they didn't come. Still, she had food prepared just in case.

Monitor and Clarify

We **monitor** comprehension to check our understanding of what we've read. We **clarify** to find out why we haven't understood what we've read and to fix up problems.

To monitor and clarify
- use background knowledge
- try different strategies: ask questions, reread, or use text features and illustrations

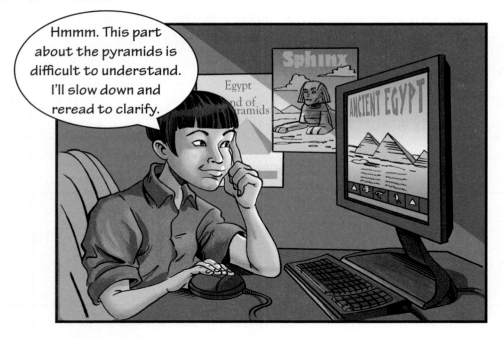

> Hmmm. This part about the pyramids is difficult to understand. I'll slow down and reread to clarify.

Let's Think About Reading!

When I monitor and clarify, I ask myself
- Do I understand what I'm reading?
- What doesn't make sense?
- What strategies can I use?

Monitor and Clarify
The Universe
by Seymour Simon

I check my understanding as I read.
If something doesn't seem to make sense, I stop reading
to find out why. Here are some notes I took on The Universe.

Confusing Information	My Thoughts
"These are two images of gas-and-dust disks forming around young stars. The disks range in size from about two to eight times the diameter of our solar system. The glow in the center of each disk is a newly formed star, about one million years old."	I thought this meant that there are stars with other stars growing inside of them. It's confusing, so I reread. It says that the images show young stars, with a circle of dust and gas around them. I look at the pictures again. . .so, the glowing part is just one star. It makes more sense now!
I am confused by the stuff about nebulas. One paragraph says, "The new stars are the bright lights inside the finger-like bulges at the top of the nebula."	What is a nebula? I scan the page to see if I can see the word "nebula" before that paragraph. Yes! It is in the second paragraph: "All stars are born within nebulas, which are eerie, dark clouds of hydrogen gas and dust." And there is a photo of a nebula, so I can see the "finger-like bulges."

Predict and Set Purpose

We **predict** to tell what might happen next in a story or article. The prediction is based on what has already happened. We **set a purpose** to guide our reading.

To predict and set a purpose
- preview the title and the author's name
- preview any illustrations or graphics
- identify why you're reading
- use what you already know to make predictions
- check and change your predictions based on new information

Let's Think About Reading!

When I predict and set a purpose, I ask myself
- What do I already know?
- What do I think will happen?
- What is my purpose for reading?

Predict and Set Purpose
Learning to Swim
by Kyoko Mori

Before I read Learning to Swim, I looked through the story to see what it might be about. I knew it had to be about the author's real life because it is an autobiography. The illustrations show a beach with what looks like a mom and daughter in bathing suits. There are also pictures of a girl swimming laps in a swimming pool. The title makes me think the story is about a girl who learns how to swim. My prediction will also be my purpose for reading.

After reading, I learned that my prediction was right. The story is about how Kyoko Mori learns to swim. Her mom is a good swimmer and teaches Kyoko the front crawl and the breaststroke. But one day a riptide carries Kyoko and her mom far from shore. They have to swim to safety on some rocks--it's scary! But the experience teaches Kyoko to be brave, and gives her confidence as a swimmer.

15

Questioning

Questioning is asking good questions about important text information. Questioning takes place before, during, and after reading.

To question

- read with a question in mind
- stop, think, and record your questions as you read
- make notes when you find information
- check your understanding and ask questions to clarify

Let's Think About Reading!

When I question, I ask myself

- Have I asked a good question with a question word?
- What questions help me make sense of my reading?
- What does the author mean?

Questioning
Don Quixote and the Windmills
retold by Eric A. Kimmel

Don Quixote and the Windmills is an exciting story, but I did have a lot of questions as I read.

Why did he change his name?

Why would a knight need a squire?

Why would Sancho Panza go with Don Quixote on his quest?

Does Don Quixote really think the windmills are giants?

Does Sancho believe what Don Quixote says?

What is the point of Don Quixote's quest?

Most of the questions I could answer in the end, but I still couldn't answer a couple of them.

1. Why would a knight need a squire? I need to look up more information about how squires helped knights in the Middle Ages, and why they would go on quests together.

2. Does Sancho believe what Don Quixote says? It's really hard to tell if Sancho believes Don Quixote, or if he is just looking for a little adventure.

Story Structure

Story structure is the arrangement of a story from beginning to end. Most stories involve a conflict and a resolution. You can use this information to summarize a story.

To identify story structure
- note the conflict, or problem, at the beginning of a story
- track the rising action as the conflict builds in the middle
- recognize the climax when the characters face the conflict
- identify how the conflict gets resolved and the story ends

Let's Think About Reading!

When I identify story structure, I ask myself
- What are the characters' goals?
- What is the story's conflict?
- How does the conflict build throughout the story?
- How is the conflict resolved in the end?

Story Structure
Good-bye to the Moon
by Monica Hughes

I read Monica Hughes's story <u>Good-bye to the Moon</u>. This is how the story structure is set up:

1) <u>Conflict</u>: Kepler Masterman is a boy who grew up on the moon. His dad is the governor there. Kepler has to move to Earth to live. He is nervous because he's never been there before!

2.) <u>Rising Action</u>: Kepler has problems with the trip on the ferry from Moon to Earth. His body isn't used to gravity, so things become tough for him the closer he gets to Earth.

3.) <u>Climax</u>: Kepler feels sick and gets a nosebleed when the ferry gets to Earth. Gravity makes him weigh more, and he has to practice walking! He is not sure he can last on Earth!

4.) <u>Resolution</u>: Kepler leaves the ferry. He notices the fluffy clouds and birds. He changes his mind and thinks that maybe life on Earth will be fun!

Summarize

We **summarize,** or retell, to check our understanding of what we've read. A summary is a brief statement—no more than a few sentences.

To summarize fiction
- tell what happens in the story
- think about the characters and their goals, the setting, and the plot

To summarize nonfiction
- tell the main idea, leaving out supporting details
- think about text structure and how the selection is organized

Let's Think About Reading!

When I summarize, I ask myself
- What is the story or selection about?
- In fiction, what are the characters' goals? Are they successful?
- In nonfiction, how is the information organized?

Summarize
The View from Saturday
by E.L. Konigsburg

When you summarize, you retell what happens in a story or an article. The summary is in your own words, and it isn't very long.

Here's my summary of The View from Saturday.

Noah's mother asks Noah to write a thank-you note to his grandprents. (He stayed with them in Florida while his parents went on a cruise.) Noah doesn't want to write the letter because he doesn't know what to thank his grandparents for.

Noah thinks about his trip. Two people where his grandparents live were getting married. Everyone had gotten together to plan the celebration. Noah helped with addressing invitations, delivering flowers, and even stood in for the injured best man!

In the end, Noah is thankful for the memory of the trip and the people he met. This helps him start writing his thank-you note!

Text Structure

We use **text structure** to look for the way the author has organized the text; for example, cause and effect, problem and solution, sequence, or compare and contrast. Analyze text structure before, during, and after reading to locate information.

To identify text structure
- before reading: preview titles, headings, and illustrations
- make predictions
- during reading: ask questions, identify the structure, and notice the organization
- after reading: recall the organization and summarize the text

Let's Think About Reading!

When I identify text structure, I ask myself
- What clues do titles, headings, and illustrations provide?
- How is information organized?
- How does the organization help my understanding?

Text Structure
Harvesting Hope
by Kathleen Krull

Harvesting Hope is a biography.
Its overall text structure is cause-and-effect.

Cause	Effect
A really bad drought destroys the 80-acre Chavez family farm in Arizona.	The family moves to California to find farm work.
Chavez hates school. It does not feel safe!	Chavez drops out of school to work all day in the fields.
Chavez sees the bad way migrant workers are often treated by farm owners.	Chavez wants to do something. He wants migrant workers to feel human and strong. He decides to dedicate his life to helping them.
Chavez organizes a march to the state capitol to fight for migrant workers' rights.	Grape company officials recognize the National Farm Workers Association and promise better conditions, including a pay raise!

Visualize

We **visualize** to form pictures in our minds as we read. This helps us monitor our comprehension.

To visualize

- combine what you already know with details from the text to make pictures in your mind
- use all of your senses to put yourself in the story or text

Let's Think About Reading!

When I visualize, I ask myself

- What do I already know?
- Which details create pictures in my mind?
- How can my senses put me in the story or text?

Visualize
Old Yeller
by Fred Gipson

When I read <u>Old Yeller</u>, I pictured a lot of the scenes in my head. For example, when Travis hears Arliss scream and then starts running through the woods to find him, I could totally picture it!

Descriptions like "the way the late sun slanted through the trees had the trail all cross-banded with streaks of bright light and dark shade" and "I ran through these bright and dark patches so fast that the changing light nearly blinded me" helped me see a woody trail at the end of the day, with trees all blurry as Travis runs past them.

I thought about all my senses (smell, sight, touch, taste, and hearing) to put myself in the scene. It was like I was right there with Travis, feeling scared and breathing hard!

Comprehension Skills

Comprehension skills are routines that you use automatically in order to better understand what you read.

As you read:

- pay attention to the way in which the text is organized.
- compare what you are reading with other things you have read.
- know what you need to look for and the ways in which to find it.
- consider the reasons why an author wrote the story or text.

Ready to Try It?

Envision It! | Visual Skills

Author's Purpose

Cause and Effect

Compare and Contrast

Draw Conclusions

Fact and Opinion

Generalize

Graphic Sources

Literary Elements

Main Idea and Details

Sequence

Author's Purpose

An author writes for many purposes, some of which are to inform, to entertain, to persuade, or to express feelings or a mood.

How to Find Author's Purpose

The author's purpose is the main reason an author has for writing a selection. Is an author writing to persuade, to inform, to entertain, or to express ideas and feelings? An author may have more than one purpose for writing.

See It!

- Before you read, look at the images. What do you see? How do the images make you feel? Why do you think those images were chosen?

- Are there a lot of subheads, text boxes, or other graphics in the selection? Why might those features be used in this text?

- Is the text bright and colorful? What about the size and shape of the words? What kind of punctuation do you notice? Does this give you an idea about the author's purpose?

Say It!

- Take turns reading aloud and listening to the first paragraph of the text with a partner.

- Discuss: What kinds of words does the author use? Do the words make it sound like he or she is trying to persuade you? What about entertain or inform? Express ideas?

- Imagine how the author's voice might sound as you read, or your partner reads aloud. Would he or she speak with a serious tone, or one more lighthearted? Why do you think so?

Do It!

- Write the author's main ideas on a piece of paper or at a computer. Examine what you wrote. What is the author trying to show?

- Draw an image of one of the author's main ideas, or use a graphic organizer like the one below.

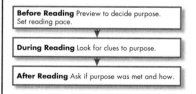

Before Reading Preview to decide purpose. Set reading pace.

During Reading Look for clues to purpose.

After Reading Ask if purpose was met and how.

- Pretend you are the author of the text, giving a "book talk." What would you say and why? Write and rehearse a short skit with a partner.

Objectives

- Identify the author's purpose.
- Draw conclusions about the text and evaluate how well the author achieves his or her purpose. • Analyze how the organization of a text affects the way ideas are related.

Envision It! | Skill Strategy

Skill

Strategy

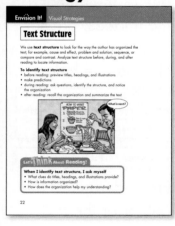

READING STREET ONLINE
ENVISION IT! ANIMATIONS
www.ReadingStreet.com

Comprehension Skill

🎯 Author's Purpose

- Authors usually write to persuade, inform, express ideas or feelings, or entertain.

- As you preview a selection, try to predict the author's purpose. After reading, ask yourself if the author met that purpose.

- Use a graphic organizer like the one below in order to determine the author's main purpose in writing "Jane Goodall's Career."

Before Reading Preview to decide purpose. Set reading pace.

⬇

During Reading Look for clues to purpose.

⬇

After Reading Ask if purpose was met and how.

Comprehension Strategy

🎯 Text Structure

Text structure is how a piece of nonfiction is organized. Types of nonfiction text structure are compare and contrast, cause and effect, sequence, and problem and solution. Sometimes titles and headings as well as bold-faced words and other features are used to organize information for the reader.

Jane Goodall's Career

Jane Goodall is known worldwide for studying chimpanzees. As a child she became interested in how animals behaved. She left school at age 18 and eventually traveled to Africa, where in 1960 she started a camp in the Gombe Stream Game Reserve. From there she could carefully research the chimpanzees that lived in the region.

Skill How do the title and first paragraph help you predict the main purpose of the article?

Goodall and her family lived in Gombe until 1975. Over the years Goodall discovered many surprising facts about chimpanzees. For example, she learned that chimpanzees are omnivores. This means that they eat both plants and animals. Before her discovery most scientists believed that chimpanzees were vegetarians, or plant eaters. Goodall also discovered that chimpanzees are capable of making and using their own tools, using twigs and the like.

Skill Do you think the author's purpose in this paragraph is to entertain, give information, or persuade?

Goodall wrote several fascinating books about her research with chimpanzees. In 1971 she told about her first years at Gombe in the book *In the Shadow of Man*. Later, in 1986, she wrote all she had learned about chimpanzee behavior in *The Chimpanzees of Gombe*.

Strategy What text structure do you think the author uses to organize information?

Your Turn!

 Need a Review? See *Envision It!* Skills and Strategies for additional help.

 **Ready to Try It?** Use what you've learned about author's purpose and text structure as you read other text.

Objectives
- Identify the author's purpose.
- Draw conclusions about a text and evaluate how well the author achieves his or her purpose.

Envision It! | Skill Strategy

Skill

Strategy

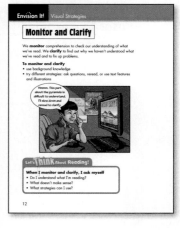

Comprehension Skill

Author's Purpose

- Authors may write to inform, persuade, express feelings or ideas, or entertain. Preview the title, headings, and pictures to help predict an author's purpose in writing something.

- When you finish reading, ask yourself, "How did the language or style help meet that purpose?"

- Make a graphic organizer like the one below in order to determine the author's main purpose in writing "The Age of Inventions."

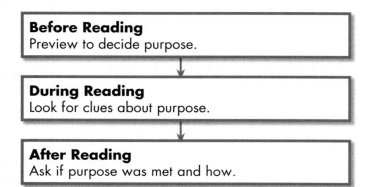

Before Reading
Preview to decide purpose.

During Reading
Look for clues about purpose.

After Reading
Ask if purpose was met and how.

Comprehension Strategy

Monitor and Clarify

Good readers make sure they understand what they are reading. If you are not sure you understand the text, stop to clarify what you have just read. If you discover, for example, that the author is giving you brand-new information using difficult words, stop and think about the meaning of each word and then reread the section that stopped you.

The Age of Inventions

The period from the mid-1800s to the early 1900s was one of great significance in human history. Many of the machines invented during this time changed the world.

First, new ways to power machines were developed. Inventors learned to generate and use electricity, leading to the widespread use of electric lights and trains. The first gasoline-fueled engine was perfected in 1859, and these engines were soon used in many factories.

Second, transportation changed dramatically. The first motorcycles and motorcars were introduced in 1855. The first large iron ships were constructed during this time as well and soon replaced ships powered by sails. The Wright brothers piloted the first plane flight in 1903.

Third, people were able to communicate in more sophisticated ways. For example, the telephone, which was made in 1876, and the wireless telegraph, invented in 1895, let people converse across long distances. The radio was invented in 1901.

The world changed in very many ways from the mid-1800s to the early 1900s. Was it a better place because of all these inventions? Many people would say yes. However, some might disagree. Transportation and communication were speedier, but noise, pollution, and a faster pace of life resulted.

Skill What do you predict is the main purpose of this article?
a) to inform you which machines were invented during this time
b) to entertain you by joking about inventions of the 1800s
c) to persuade you that this time was very popular

Strategy Are you understanding the author's purpose and the information in the article? Do you need to stop and think?

Skill What does the purpose of this final paragraph seem to be—to inform, to entertain, or to express ideas?

Your Turn!

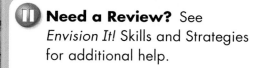 **Need a Review?** See *Envision It!* Skills and Strategies for additional help.

Ready to Try It? Use what you've learned about author's purpose and monitoring and clarifying as you read other text.

Objectives
● Draw conclusions about texts and evaluate how well the author achieves his or her purpose. ● Understand how to use the questioning strategy to comprehend text.

Envision It! Skill Strategy

Skill

Strategy

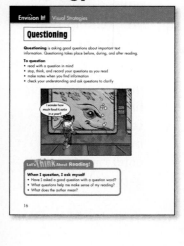

READING STREET ONLINE
ENVISION IT! ANIMATIONS
www.ReadingStreet.com

Comprehension Skill

Author's Purpose

- Authors have different reasons for writing. They may write to persuade, inform, entertain, or express thoughts and feelings. They may have more than one purpose for writing.

- Study what the author writes to help you figure out his or her purpose for writing.

- Adjust the way you read based on the author's purpose. If the purpose is to entertain, you may read faster. If the purpose is to inform, you may want to read more slowly.

- Use a graphic organizer like the one below to determine the author's purpose for writing "Gina's Adventures in Italy."

Comprehension Strategy

Questioning

Active readers ask frequent questions before, during, and after reading. You can ask a literal question, which can be answered by looking at or recalling information directly from the text. Inferential or interpretive questions may lead you to do more thinking, discussion, or even research about what you are reading.

Gina's Adventures in Italy

My sister Gina has always been unique. She repeatedly showed this during the summer we spent in Italy.

In Florence, Gina was admiring a row of scooters parked on the sidewalk. In typical Gina fashion, she accidentally bumped into one, and they all fell like a row of dominoes. Later I suggested we go see Michelangelo's famous sculpture, *David*. "David who? Do we know this fellow?" Gina asked. As always, I gave up trying to explain and just took her there. She loved it.

Our next stop was Rome. I had always wanted to see the Trevi Fountain, the gorgeous old fountain that many tourists wade in on hot days. Gina had obviously heard about this because, as we walked toward the fountain, I saw her donning a bathing cap and swim goggles. "What are you doing?" I asked.

"I read that you can go in. I'm having a swim!" she said. I watched as she galloped to the fountain and jumped in. Other tourists watched the strange scene with amazement. "Man, I wish I had my flippers!" Gina said as she came up for air.

Strategy What questions can you ask before reading that will help you understand this story?

Skill How do you know that the purpose of this paragraph is to entertain you by describing some silly situations, rather than to inform you about scooters in Florence or the works of Michelangelo?

Skill Which details in this paragraph tell you that its purpose is to entertain you?

Your Turn!

⏸ **Need a Review?** See *Envision It!* Skills and Strategies for additional help.

▶ **Ready to Try It?** Use what you've learned about author's purpose and questioning as you read other text.

Cause and Effect

An effect is something that happens. A cause is why that thing happens. Clue words such as *because*, *as a result*, *therefore*, and *so that* can signal causes and effects.

Cause

Effect

How to Identify Cause and Effect

A cause is what makes something happen. An effect is something that happens as a result of a cause. A cause may have more than one effect, and an effect may have more than one cause.

See It!

- Look for clue words in a text, such as *because, so, since, then,* and *for that reason.*

- Make a picture in your mind as you read the sentence: *Nicole spilled a glass of water on the floor. Jeff walked into the room and slipped on the spill.* Identify the cause by answering, "What happened first?" Identify the effect by answering, "What happened afterward?"

- Search for clues in the illustrations of a story that might tell you about what happened and why.

Say It!

- To find a cause, ask yourself or a partner, "Why did this happen?" To find an effect, ask, "What happened because of this?"

- Take turns telling a partner what happened in a story, and how it happened.

- Listen to a partner read sentences or paragraphs from your reading aloud. Try to hear clue words, such as *because* or *so,* that tell about cause and effect.

Do It!

- Write an effect to the following cause: *The temperature dropped to 40 degrees Fahrenheit when we were outside.*

- Make a graphic organizer like the one below to find cause-and-effect relationships in your reading:

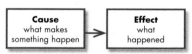

- Write "what" and "why" questions about what you have read to a partner. Have your partner answer aloud or in writing.

Objectives
- Analyze how the organization of a text, such as cause-and-effect, affects the way ideas are related.
- Identify effects and their causes.
- Summarize the main ideas and supporting details in a text.

Envision It! | Skill / Strategy

Skill

Strategy

Comprehension Skill

Cause and Effect

- A cause is what makes something happen. An effect is something that happens as a result of a cause. To find a cause, ask yourself, "Why did this happen?" To find an effect, ask yourself, "What happened because of this?"

- Clue words such as *because, so,* and *due to* can help you spot cause-and-effect relationships.

- Make a graphic organizer like the one below to note cause-and-effect relationships as you read "The Arctic."

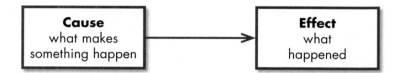

| **Cause** what makes something happen | → | **Effect** what happened |

Comprehension Strategy

Important Ideas

Important ideas in a nonfiction text are often set off in different typefaces, with signal words, or by the use of other text features, such as capital letters, that can guide the reader to better understanding.

THE ARCTIC

THE ARCTIC is located on the northernmost part of Earth. It is often considered to lie north of the "tree line," which marks where trees cannot grow because of frigid year-round temperatures. This area includes Greenland as well as parts of Alaska, Canada, Europe, and Siberia. It also includes the Arctic Ocean and, of course, the North Pole.

Ice and snow cover two-fifths of arctic land year-round, while the rest of the land has grasses and shrubs. Ice covers more than half the Arctic Ocean all the time. This mass of jagged ice is called pack ice.

THERE ARE LARGE temperature differences throughout the Arctic. Due to Earth's tilt, the sun's rays do not even reach the northern Arctic during the winter. Yet the coldest arctic temperatures are not at the North Pole. That's because the North Pole is located on the Arctic Ocean pack ice. Water—even as ice—slowly takes in heat during the summer. It slowly gives it off during the winter. The most extreme temperatures, then, occur on the land in northern Canada, Alaska, and Siberia.

On the pack ice, winter air is still and dry. Most of the water is already frozen. In fact, more snow falls in New York City!

Skill Clue words such as *due to* help you spot cause-and-effect relationships. Why don't the sun's rays reach the northern Arctic in winter?

Skill Why aren't the coldest temperatures at the North Pole?

Strategy What are the most important ideas in this article? Summarize the article to state its most important ideas.

Your Turn!

 Need a Review? See *Envision It! Skills and Strategies* for additional help.

Ready to Try It? Use what you've learned about cause and effect and important ideas as you read other text.

Objectives

• Analyze how the organization of a text, such as cause-and-effect, affects the way ideas are related.

• Understand and make inferences about a nonfiction text and provide evidence from the text to support understanding.

Envision It! | **Skill Strategy**

Skill

Strategy

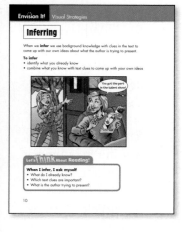

Comprehension Skill

Cause and Effect

• A cause is what makes something happen. An effect is something that happens as a result of a cause. Several causes may lead to one effect.

• Clue words and phrases such as *consequently, as a result,* and *therefore* can help you spot cause-and-effect relationships. Sometimes, though, there are no clue words.

• Use a graphic organizer like the one below to organize causes and effects you find in "Goodbye, Jim Crow."

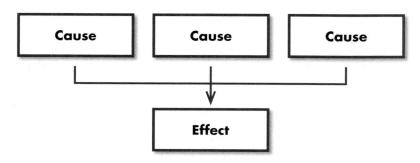

Comprehension Strategy

Inferring

Authors do not always tell you everything you need to know to understand what you are reading. You may need to add information you already know— your prior knowledge—in order to make inferences, or figure out what is happening in a text. Active readers infer about ideas and meanings to help them understand what they are reading.

GOODBYE, JIM CROW

It took many years for black people to receive full legal rights in the United States. The push for fair laws began after the Civil War ended.

• **Unfair Laws** Starting in 1865, a group of laws called black codes stopped blacks from having basic rights. Citizens in the northern part of the United States disagreed with these laws. This led to the Reconstruction laws, which got rid of the black codes. But soon new laws were passed that segregated, or separated, blacks from whites in many areas of everyday life. These were called the Jim Crow laws.

• **New Laws** In 1954, the United States Supreme Court ruled that it was not fair or lawful to have separate black and white schools. This helped the Civil Rights movement move forward with a strong, organized push to end segregation. In 1963, leaders of the movement staged a huge march in Washington, D.C., to speak out against racial discrimination.

President Kennedy could not get Congress to pass equal rights laws. After President Kennedy was assassinated, President Johnson got Congress to pass the Civil Rights Act of 1964, which ended legal segregation. Then, in 1965, Congress passed the Voting Rights Act. This led to a huge increase in the number of blacks registered to vote.

Strategy Use your ability to infer to answer this question: Why did the Civil Rights movement start *after* the Civil War ended?
a) Once the war ended, slaves were free.
b) There wasn't interest on the part of black people until then.
c) Before the war, discrimination was illegal.

Skill What caused the United States to pass the Reconstruction laws? Are there clue words?

Skill What was the long-term effect of the important 1954 Supreme Court decision?

Your Turn!

Need a Review? See *Envision It!* Skills and Strategies for additional help.

 Ready to Try It? Use what you've learned about cause and effect and inferring as you read other text.

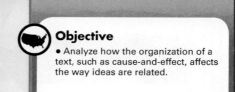

Objective

● Analyze how the organization of a text, such as cause-and-effect, affects the way ideas are related.

Envision It! | Skill Strategy

Skill

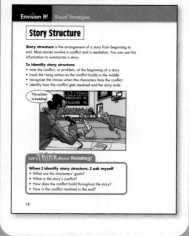

Strategy

Comprehension Skill

Cause and Effect

- A cause is what makes something happen. An effect is something that can happen as the result of a cause. Clue words such as *since, thus, as a result, therefore,* and *consequently* point to cause-and-effect relationships.

- Sometimes an effect has more than one cause; sometimes one cause has more than one effect.

- When a cause is not directly stated, you must think about why something happened.

- Use a graphic organizer like the one below to identify cause and effect as you read the tall tale "Super Smart."

Comprehension Strategy

Story Structure

Active readers pay attention to the story structure of fiction. In most writing, a story has a beginning, when characters and the plot are introduced; a middle, when problems or conflicts are introduced; and an end or climax, when the problems or conflicts are resolved. Authors may also use story incidents to foreshadow or hint at future events.

Super Smart

Long ago and far away lived Super Smart. The day she was born, her mother said, "Here are six diapers."

"Here are three more," said her father. When the baby held up nine tiny fingers, he said, "She is super smart!" And that is how she got her name.

The next day, her father started to read her a story. When he pointed to a picture, Super Smart read the whole page out loud. She read book after book, so fast that her mother and father kept running out of books.

Super Smart's parents were glad when she was old enough to go to school. They were tired of buying books. But the first week of school, Super Smart read all the books in the school.

Next, Super Smart started reading her way through the library. In a month, she had read all the books in the library.

"That's okay," said Super Smart. "These books are too easy anyway. I will write books for smart people so I will have something to read."

So Super Smart started writing books. She wrote so many that a whole new bigger library had to be built. Unfortunately, nobody else was smart enough to read her books. And that is why none of her books are read today.

Skill Describe what earned Super Smart her name.

Skill Why did Super Smart start writing books?

Strategy What did you learn at the beginning, middle, and end of this story?

Your Turn!

 Need a Review? See *Envision It!* Skills and Strategies for additional help.

Ready to Try It?
Use what you've learned about cause and effect and story structure as you read other text.

Compare and Contrast

To compare and contrast is to look for similarities and differences in things. Clue words such as *like* or *as* show similarities. Clue words such as *but* or *unlike* show differences.

How to Compare and Contrast

When we compare things, we say what is similar about them. When we contrast things, we say what is different. During reading, we think about what is alike and what is different. Implicit comparisons don't use clue words. You have to figure out for yourself that two or more things are alike or different.

See It!

- Look at the picture on page 44. What does it tell you about comparing and contrasting?

- Look at the illustrations that go with the story you are reading. Compare and contrast the characters, animals, and various settings that you see.

- Look for clues words such as *like, as,* and *same* that signal two things are similar. Look for words such as *but, unlike,* and *different* to show differences.

Say It!

- Tell a partner how you are alike and different from a family member. For example: *My brother is loud and talkative, but I am shy and quiet. However, we both like to play baseball.*

- As you read, stop at parts of the story that might describe things that are similar or different. Explain these similarities or differences to a partner.

- Name an item in the classroom. Have a partner tell you one thing in the room that is similar to that object, one thing that is different, and why.

Do It!

- Make a Venn diagram like the one below for telling how characters are alike or different:

- With your teacher, gather small items around the room that you can compare and contrast. How are the things you've chosen alike? How are they different?

- Compare and contrast something in nature, and make an illustrated book of your results. Write labels for your illustrations that tell how things are alike or different.

Objectives

• Analyze how the organization of a text, such as compare-and-contrast, affects the way ideas are related.

• Summarize the main ideas and supporting details in a text.

Envision It! Skill Strategy

Skill

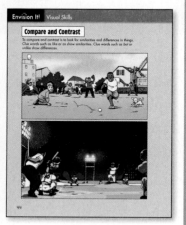

Strategy

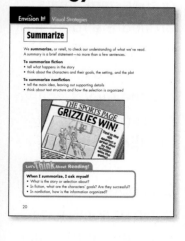

**READING STREET ONLINE
ENVISION IT! ANIMATIONS
www.ReadingStreet.com**

Comprehension Skill

Compare and Contrast

• When you compare and contrast, you tell how two or more things are alike and different.

• Clue words such as *like* or *as* show similarities. Clue words such as *but* or *unlike* show differences.

• You can also sum up differences and similarities between two things or people as in this example: *James is quiet while Juanita is outgoing, but they both like sports.*

• Make a graphic organizer like the one below to compare and contrast Marville and Abbey Creek as you read "This New Town."

Marville
Trait
Trait

Both
Trait
Trait

Abbey Creek
Trait
Trait

Comprehension Strategy

Summarize

Good readers understand text better when they summarize, or briefly state, the most important ideas in a selection. When you summarize something, use your own words, or paraphrase, and focus on main ideas rather than on details.

46

This New Town

It's been a year since we moved to Abbey Creek. I am still getting acquainted with my new town.

In Marville, we could play outside even after dusk. All summer long we'd play games in the street. There weren't many cars to be concerned about. Because there is so much traffic in Abbey Creek, we play in the yards instead of the street. The yards in Marville were really spacious. The yards here are like postage stamps.

Skill What does comparing the yards to postage stamps tell you about the yards?

In some ways, though, Abbey Creek is superior to Marville. The houses here are more interesting. Each one is unique. In Marville, the houses all looked similar. There are more places to visit here. There are convenience stores and comic book shops. Abbey Creek is like a carnival; Marville was like a golf course.

Skill Compare the houses in the two towns. How are they different?

Despite the differences, the two towns have things in common. Both of them have outstanding schools. Each town's park district offers a lot of classes and sports. Abbey Creek has a terrific public library just like Marville did. And, like Marville, it has a lot of kids, although I'm not familiar with all of them yet.

Strategy Summarize why Abbey Creek is superior to Marville. Then summarize how the two places are similar.

Your Turn!

Need a Review? See *Envision It!* Skills and Strategies for additional help.

Ready to Try It? Use what you've learned about comparing and contrasting and summarizing as you read other text.

Objectives
• Analyze how the organization of a text, such as compare-and-contrast, affects the way ideas are related.
• Use story structure to understand a text.

Envision It! | Skill Strategy

Skill

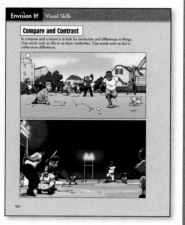

Strategy

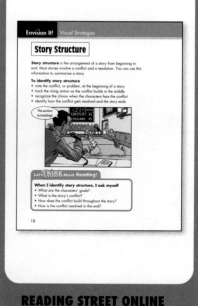

Comprehension Skill

◎ Compare and Contrast

- To compare and contrast means to tell how two or more things are alike and different.

- Clue words such as *like* or *as* show similarities. Words such as *unlike* and *however* show differences.

- Ask questions while you read to compare and contrast, such as "How are these two characters alike and different?" or "What does this situation remind me of?"

- Use a graphic organizer like the one below to compare and contrast Anna and Charlie in "My Siblings."

Character X
Trait
Trait

Both
Trait
Trait

Character Y
Trait
Trait

Comprehension Strategy

◎ Story Structure

Recognizing story structure will help you understand how the components fit together to form a framework for the story.

48

My Siblings

My older sibling is Anna, and my younger sibling is Charlie. We all come from the same family, but Anna and Charlie are like night and day.

Anna is 13, and I've never seen a better worker. She is as efficient and orderly as a perfectly programmed robot and can multitask like you wouldn't believe. Anna can clean her room while doing her homework and talking on the phone. Everything she does turns out great. Sometimes I think that Anna is a powerful computer that has somehow acquired a human body.

Then there's Charlie, a very different species. It's clear to everyone in the family that he's from another planet. Charlie is the most imaginative creature I know. Despite being only 6 years old, he can build fabulous structures out of blocks, invent weird and wonderful games, and make up odd words and names. His mind is like a swarm of bees—constantly moving and swirling. He is a walking tornado, always leaving gigantic, complex messes in his wake. Kind? Yes—but as unique as they come.

What about me, you ask? Well, I'm nothing like either of them.

Skill Based on the phrase *like night and day*, do you think that Anna and Charlie are similar? Why or why not?

Strategy The structure of the story uses description to tell about the characters. How else is the story arranged?

Skill Here is one point of contrast: how Anna and Charlie affect the family home. How are they different?

Your Turn!

 Need a Review? See *Envision It!* Skills and Strategies for additional help.

 Ready to Try It? Use what you've learned about comparing and contrasting and story structure as you read other text.

Envision It! | Skill Strategy

Skill

Strategy

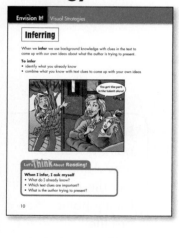

READING STREET ONLINE
ENVISION IT! ANIMATIONS
www.ReadingStreet.com

Comprehension Skill

Compare and Contrast

When you compare and contrast, you tell how two or more things are alike or different.

- Clue words such as *like*, *similarly*, and *both* can show comparison. Clue words such as *unlike*, *on the other hand*, and *however* can indicate contrast.

- Sometimes writers do not use clue words.

- Use a graphic organizer like the one below to compare and contrast Mrs. Wallen and Mrs. Casa in "My Fifth-Grade Teachers."

Person A
characteristic
characteristic

Both
characteristic
characteristic

Person B
characteristic
characteristic

Comprehension Strategy

Inferring

Authors do not always tell readers everything about the characters, setting, and events in a story. For better understanding, readers need to infer, or figure out on their own, what is not stated directly. Use details from the text and from your own experiences to make inferences about the ideas, themes, and lessons of a written work as you read.

50

My Fifth-Grade Teachers

When I was in fifth grade, our school combined two classes together in one extra-large classroom. We were co-taught by two teachers, Mrs. Wallen and Mrs. Casa.

Mrs. Wallen was very strict. She had clear procedures for everything, from how you stood in line to how you raised your hand. She tended to be serious and curt. But she expected a lot from us and made sure we learned everything we were supposed to learn. Mrs. Wallen's appearance was flawless. Her blond hair was always perfectly done. Her clothes were always carefully pressed, and her posture was always perfect. She was like a well-dressed statue.

Mrs. Casa, on the other hand, was a lot softer. She had a wonderful sense of humor and enjoyed a little playful banter during lessons. However, if we ever got out of control or lost our focus, she would very strongly bring us back to attention. She was inconsistent at enforcing the rules but always insisted that we work hard, pay attention, and learn. Well-dressed and pretty, she was a welcome sight each morning.

Despite their differences, Mrs. Casa and Mrs. Wallen worked well together. They were both great teachers, and I learned a lot that year.

Skill When the author says Mrs. Wallen is *like a well-dressed statue,* in what way are a statue and Mrs. Wallen alike?
a) They both have perfect posture.
b) They both are made of stone.
c) They both are very strict.

Skill In what ways are the two teachers alike and different? Look back at the descriptions of each. Do you see any clue words that might help you compare and contrast them?

Strategy With which teacher would you expect the students to have more fun? What details from the story tell you? How does your own experience support your inference?

Your Turn!

❚❚ Need a Review? See *Envision It!* Skills and Strategies for additional help.

▶ Ready to Try It? Use what you've learned about comparing and contrasting and inferring as you read other text.

Draw Conclusions

When we draw conclusions, we make sensible decisions or form reasonable opinions after thinking about the facts and details in what we are reading.

How to Draw Conclusions

When we draw conclusions, we form a reasonable opinion about something we have read. We combine our own background knowledge with the facts and details stated in a text to make these inferences.

See It!

- Look at page 52. What details do you notice? What conclusions can you make about what is happening? Explain.

- Look at the illustrations that go with your reading. How does what you see help you draw conclusions about the story? What sort of information do the images reveal?

- Picture in your mind someone who is mad, happy, sad, or excited. What sort of clues do they give you about their mood?

Say It!

- If stuck when asked to draw a conclusion, go back and quietly read aloud places where you might find facts and details that support a particular conclusion.

- Share with a small group what you already know about a subject. Each group member should share his or her knowledge about the subject. This information can help you draw conclusions.

- Ask "Why is this happening?" as you read. With a partner, talk through the conclusions you make. Ask "Is this the only logical conclusion?"

Do It!

- Make a graphic organizer like the one below to help you draw conclusions.

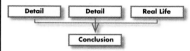

- Write a brief mystery story in which the main character has to draw a conclusion based on clues. Make sure to include facts and details that help the character solve the mystery.

- Write "Who or What Am I?" questions for a partner. Give your partner three facts or details about something, and ask him or her to draw a conclusion based on the information.

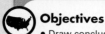

Objectives
- Draw conclusions from the information presented by an author.

Envision It! | Skill Strategy

Skill

Strategy

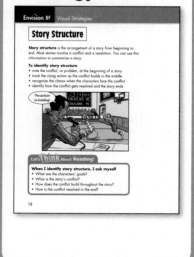

Comprehension Skill

Draw Conclusions

- When you draw a conclusion, you form a reasonable opinion about something you have read. Drawing conclusions is related to making inferences, or inferring.

- Use what you know about real life to help you draw conclusions.

- When you draw a conclusion, it should make sense. Ask *Is my conclusion based on facts?* or *Does what I have read support my conclusion?*

- As you read the selection, use a graphic organizer like the one below to help you draw a conclusion about why the author titled the selection "Twice Lost; Twice Won."

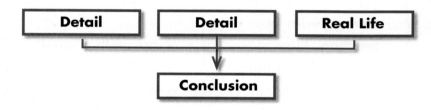

| Detail | Detail | Real Life |

Conclusion

Comprehension Strategy

Story Structure

A fictional story is often arranged sequentially, or in the order that events happen. Plot is important to a story's structure: the problem, the rising action, the climax, and the outcome or resolution to the problem make up the plot.

TWICE LOST; TWICE WON

My little brother raced into my room shouting, "I lost another tooth!"

I knew this was big news to him, but it was not the high point of my day. Still, I wanted to show my support. "Great! Don't forget to put it under your pillow tonight." I watched my brother slide the tooth into his shirt pocket and head to the hall. Then I went back to studying for my test.

Time flew, and I was getting ready to head out for the big basketball game when my brother dashed back into my room. This time, his eyes were red. He sniffled and hung his head. "I lost it," he said.

"Lost what?" I asked, knowing that I'd have to pack up my uniform and head for the basketball court soon. I hoped this was no big disaster. I couldn't miss the playoff game, and I knew my little brother was looking forward to it too.

"My tooth! I lost my tooth."

I looked at the clock—fifteen minutes until I had to leave. "Okay, where's your shirt, the one you were wearing when you came into my room earlier?"

He led me to a pile of clothes on his closet floor. I rummaged through them but found no tooth. By this time, my brother was sobbing. Then I had an idea. "Where were you when you changed clothes?" I asked.

"In the laundry room," came the muffled reply.

With three minutes to spare, we raced to the laundry room. There, back in a corner, was my brother's tooth. As it turned out, I won twice that day!

Strategy What is the problem of the story? How do you think it will be resolved?

Skill Based on this paragraph, what conclusion can you draw about the main character's basketball game? Explain.

Skill What can you conclude about where the tooth might be?

Your Turn!

 Need a Review? See *Envision It! Skills and Strategies* for additional help.

▶ **Ready to Try It?** Use what you've learned about drawing conclusions and story structure as you read other text.

Objectives

• Explore, create ideas, and come to conclusions about descriptive writing and show proof from the text to support your conclusions.
• Set a purpose for reading a text based on what you hope to get from the text.

Envision It! | Skill Strategy

Skill

Strategy

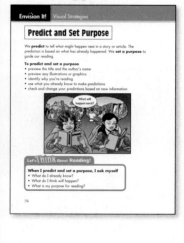

READING STREET ONLINE
ENVISION IT! ANIMATIONS
www.ReadingStreet.com

Comprehension Skill

Draw Conclusions

• When you draw a conclusion, you form a reasonable opinion about what you have read. Use what you know about real life to help you draw conclusions.

• Be sure that there are enough facts and pieces of information in the text to support your conclusions.

• Make a graphic organizer like the one below to help you come to a valid conclusion as you read the letter from Lydia to Rachel on the next page.

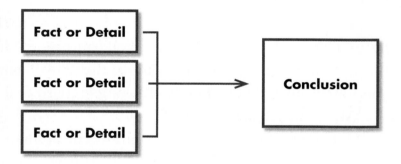

Comprehension Strategy

Predict and Set Purpose

Good readers try to predict the kinds of facts or details they will find in the text. Doing this helps to set a purpose for reading. When you have predicted what you will read, go back after you finish reading to see if you were correct.

56

March 12, 2011
1221 Sea Gull Way
Gulliver, Florida

Dear Rachel,

How are you? It has been ten weeks now since we moved to Florida so my mom could do her ocean research. Our new town is very different from New York. It doesn't snow here, and the temperature is too hot for me.

There's not much going on in this area, and there aren't very many places to go other than the beach. We live in a very small town near the ocean. There's not much to do most of the time, but sometimes I get to go with my mom when she does her research, and that's great. Still, I miss all the activity and all the people in the big city. Remember how we used to go to shows and get the best pizza slices? There's a lot of seafood to eat here, which is pretty gross since I don't like it. It is so much fun where you are, where there is always something to do.

My new school is called Marina Bay School. Last week, we were studying the ocean, and my mom came to give a presentation. That made me feel like I fit in a little bit better with some of the kids in this new town.

At recess, I usually sort of sit on the sidelines and watch the other kids play volleyball or kickball. There's no one like you here. Are you doing all right? Are you still racing with Ellen and Juanita at recess like we used to? That was awesome!

Sincerely,
Lydia

Strategy What do you predict this letter will be about? What purpose will you set for reading?

Skill Which conclusion can you draw about Lydia's view of her new home?
a) She felt more comfortable in New York.
b) She wishes things were quieter where she lives now.
c) She likes her new home better than her old home.

Skill What conclusion can you draw about how Lydia is feeling?

Your Turn!

 Need a Review? See *Envision It!* Skills and Strategies for additional help.

 Ready to Try It? Use what you've learned about drawing conclusions and predicting and setting a purpose as you read other text.

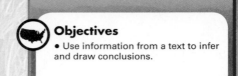

Objectives

● Use information from a text to infer and draw conclusions.

Envision It! | Skill Strategy

Skill

Strategy

Comprehension Skill

Draw Conclusions

- When you draw a conclusion, you form a reasonable opinion about something you have read.

- Ask yourself if your conclusions are valid. Do the facts and details in the text support your conclusions? Is each conclusion valid, based on logical thinking and common sense?

- Use a graphic organizer like the one below to help you draw a conclusion about the character traits of the people who are written about in "The Conquistadores."

- Evaluate your conclusion by answering these questions: What facts or details support your conclusion? Is your conclusion based on common sense and logical thinking? Explain.

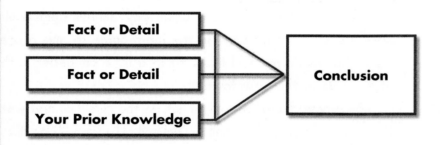

Fact or Detail	
Fact or Detail	**Conclusion**
Your Prior Knowledge	

Comprehension Strategy

Important Ideas

You can better understand a selection if you look for its important ideas. The important ideas are the text's essential information, facts, and details. The title gives clues to the topic. A topic sentence tells what each paragraph is about. Reading topic sentences first can guide you to important ideas.

The Conquistadores

During the 1500s, Spaniards sailed to the Americas and began to explore the land they found. In time, some of them began to conquer and take control over parts of the Americas. These Spaniards were called *conquistadores,* which is the Spanish word for "conquerors." These men were arguably most interested in fighting and searching for gold.

Francisco Pizarro is known for conquering the Inca people of South America. In 1531, Pizarro set sail for the center of the mighty Inca empire. He had with him 180 men and nearly 40 horses. The Incas had a much larger army, but they were fighting among themselves. Pizarro and his men made a surprise attack against the Incas and captured their leader. Later, this leader was killed by Pizarro's men, even after he gave the Spaniards a room full of gold and silver.

Sebastián de Belalcázar, another conquistador, helped Pizarro conquer the Incas. In 1534, he led a small army that attacked and occupied the valley of Quito, a former capital. History demonstrates that most of the conquistadores were better at fighting than governing. Because of this, other Spanish leaders eventually took their places.

Strategy What important idea about the conquistadores is expressed in this paragraph?

Skill Which of the following conclusions about Pizarro is valid? Think about his actions.

a) He was generous.
b) He was clever.
c) He was afraid.

Skill Draw a conclusion in order to answer the following question: What do you think the conquistadores were like as rulers?

Your Turn!

 Need a Review? See *Envision It!* Skills and Strategies for additional help.

▶ **Ready to Try It?** Use what you've learned about drawing conclusions and important ideas as you read other text.

Fact and Opinion

A fact is something that can be proved. Facts are based on evidence. Opinions express ideas and are based on the interpretation of evidence.

How to Identify Fact and Opinion

A statement of fact can be proven true or false by reading, observing, or asking an expert. A statement of opinion cannot be proven true or false. Opinions tell someone's ideas or feelings, and should be supported by good logic.

See It!

- Look at the picture on page 60. What fact is given? How do you know this is a fact? What opinion is given? How do you know?

- Look at reference books such as encyclopedias, textbooks, or official Web sites to find out if a statement is true or false. Some sentences will contain both facts and opinions.

- Look for clue words that something is an opinion. They include words such as *favorite, great, exciting,* and *boring.*

Say It!

- Tell one fact and one opinion about something you know about. Your partner should identify which statement is a fact and which is an opinion.

- State an opinion, such as: *Soccer is the best sport to play.* A partner should change your statement to one that tells a fact or supports the opinion with details. *(It is the best sport because ...).*

- Read the following aloud, and tell which is fact, and which is opinion:
1. *It's too cold in here!*
2. *The thermometer says it is 30 degrees Fahrenheit.*

Do It!

- Use a graphic organizer such as the one below to help you organize the facts and valid opinions in a text.

Statement	Fact? How Can It Be Checked?	Opinion? What Are Clue Words?

- Write a paragraph about what you did in the morning before school. Be sure to include facts and opinions.

- Ask for permission to look at classroom books. Record what facts or opinions you read. How can you tell what is fact and what is opinion? Explain your reasoning.

Objectives
- Identify the facts in a text and prove that they are facts. • Distinguish between a faulty and a valid opinion.

Envision It! | Skill Strategy

Skill

Strategy

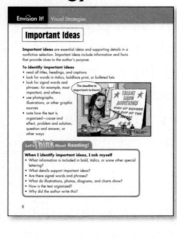

Comprehension Skill

Fact and Opinion

- A statement that can be proved true or false is called a fact.

- A statement that tells a person's thoughts, feelings, or ideas is called an opinion. Opinions cannot be proved true or false.

- Opinions may be either valid or faulty. Valid opinions are supported by facts or are stated by experts. Faulty opinions are not supported by facts, experts, or logic; they might be based on a false statement of fact.

- Use a graphic organizer like the one below as you read "Give the Oceans a Break!"

Statement of Opinion	Support	Valid or Faulty
Statement	Fact or Expert knowledge	Valid
Statement	none	Faulty

Comprehension Strategy

 Important Ideas

Good readers pay close attention to the important ideas in a piece of writing. Important ideas are sometimes set off in a different typeface or are found in graphics that show the essential ideas and supporting details. Finding important ideas helps readers understand what an author is writing about.

Give the Oceans a Break!

Why do humans harm the oceans when oceans are so important to them?

The oceans provide humans with many important things, such as fish. Overall, humans really like fish. Each year millions of tons of ocean fish are caught and eaten by humans.

The oceans are also a source of energy. Millions of barrels of oil are pumped from the oceans each day. Energy from oceans is important because if we didn't have it, we would not have electricity.

The most important thing humans get from the oceans is minerals. My friend Tom, who lives near the ocean, says, "The ocean gives us sand, gravel, and sometimes even gold and silver."

But humans have really harmed the oceans. Many areas of the oceans have been heavily polluted by raw sewage, garbage, and toxic chemicals. In other areas, the fertilizers and pesticides that humans use enter the oceans and make it harder for sea animals to survive.

Overfishing has also hurt sea life. The populations of many sea creatures have declined over the years because of humans' fishing. I think all ocean fishing should be illegal.

I think it's time we took better care of our oceans.

Skill Is this statement a valid opinion, or a faulty opinion? Why?

Strategy In your own words, what is the important idea in this paragraph?

Skill How can you tell whether this opinion is faulty or valid?

Your Turn!

 Need a Review? See *Envision It!* Skills and Strategies for additional help.

▶ **Ready to Try It?** Use what you've learned about fact and opinion and important ideas as you read other text.

Objectives
• Identify the facts in a text and prove that they are facts.
• Explore, create ideas, and come to conclusions about informative and descriptive writing and show proof from the text to support your research.

Envision It! | Skill Strategy

Skill

Strategy

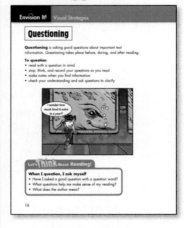

Comprehension Skill

Fact and Opinion

• Facts can be proved true or false by reading, observing, or asking an expert.

• Opinions are judgments or beliefs. They cannot be proved true or false, but they can be supported by facts and logic.

• Sometimes one statement expresses both a fact and an opinion.

• Use a graphic organizer like the one below to identify facts and opinions in "Dogs Versus Cats."

Statement	Fact? How Can It Be Checked?	Opinion? What Are Clue Words?

Comprehension Strategy

Questioning

You will better understand what you are reading if you ask questions about important text information before, during, and after you read. Record questions as you develop them. Make a note when you find information that answers your questions.

DOGS Versus CATS

Doug and Rose heard Biscuit barking frantically as they walked up the path. His friendly face looked out eagerly from the front window. As they entered, Biscuit bounded toward them, his tail a blur. He raced from Doug to Rose and then around in circles.

Skill Which sentence in this paragraph states an opinion?

Mittens slept curled up on the sofa. Rose sat beside her and stroked her fur. Mittens purred loudly. Then she stood up, stretched, and walked away. "Dogs are much better pets than cats," said Doug, scratching Biscuit's ears. Biscuit licked his hand.

"No, they aren't!" said Rose.

Strategy What question could a reader ask at this point?

Doug said, "Biscuit always runs to meet us. Mittens stays where she is. If we go to her, sometimes she lets us pet her and sometimes she doesn't. Biscuit follows us everywhere and always wants to please us."

"Dogs can be pests. Biscuit always wants attention," said Rose. "He barks at every person or dog that passes by."

Skill Find a fact and an opinion in this paragraph.

"It's better to have a pet that thinks I am wonderful and that is always there for me," said Doug.

"It's better to have a pet that is quiet, independent, and leaves me alone sometimes," said Rose.

"I guess it all depends on what you prefer in a pet," said Doug. "They're both good choices."

Your Turn!

❚❚ Need a Review? See *Envision It!* Skills and Strategies for additional help.

▶ Ready to Try It? Use what you've learned about fact and opinion and questioning as you read other text.

Objectives
● Understand the difference between facts and opinions. Evaluate statements of opinion. ● Analyze how the organization of a text affects the ways ideas are related.

Envision It! | Skill Strategy

Skill

Strategy

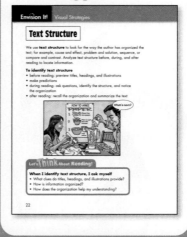

Comprehension Skill

Fact and Opinion

- Careful readers watch for statements of opinion as they read. While facts can be proved true or false, opinions cannot be proved. They can, however, be shown to be valid or faulty.

- Valid statements of opinion can be supported by facts, experts or logic. Faulty statements of opinion cannot be supported.

- Use a graphic organizer like the one below to evaluate the opinions stated in "The Best Job in the World."

Opinion	Source	Valid or Faulty

Comprehension Strategy

Text Structure

Text structure is the way a piece of writing is organized. External organization includes titles and headings, special typefaces, and various illustrations and graphics. Internal organization is the way that the writer structures thoughts and ideas. Internal methods of organization include using compare and contrast, cause and effect, sequence, and description.

The Best Job IN THE WORLD

Movers transport people's belongings from one location to another. Movers have the best job in the world because they are healthy, they get to help people every day, and they get to see many interesting places.

Strategy How can you tell that this writer is using description to organize the text?

Movers use their muscles when they work. I think exercising your muscles makes you strong. Movers are the strongest workers in the world because they use their muscles more than anything

Skill Which of the following tells you that this statement of opinion is faulty?
a) It is based only on someone's opinion.
b) It was stated by an expert.
c) It is based on incorrect facts.

Movers have the best job because each day they get to help other people, and that makes movers happy. I think movers are happy because Dr. David Kell recently did a study showing that helpful people tend to be happier. Everyone enjoys helping others. Think of how nice it would be to do so all day, every day.

Finally, movers always get to see new and interesting places. Office workers who sit at their desks each day can't say that. Movers get to see mansions, unique apartments, and other types of living places. That is always fun to do.

Skill Is the author's statement of opinion well supported or poorly supported?

In conclusion, movers have the best job in the world because they exercise, help others, and get to see new places every day. Now, don't you want to be a mover?

Your Turn!

Need a Review? See *Envision It!* Skills and Strategies for additional help.

Ready to Try It? Use what you've learned about fact and opinion and text structure as you read other text.

Generalize

To generalize is to make a broad statement or rule that applies to many examples.

How to Generalize

A generalization is a broad statement about something that applies to many examples. When you are given ideas about several things or people and you make a statement that applies to all of them, you are generalizing.

See It!

- Look at the picture on page 68. What does it tell you about making generalizations?

- As you read, look for clue words that might signal a generalization, such as *many, most, usually, never, all,* or *few.*

- Look around the classroom for objects you can make a generalization about. When you have chosen an object, examine it and make a generalization. Remember to ask yourself if your generalization can be supported by facts.

Say It!

- As you read, look for words or phrases that make broad statements about someone or something. When you find such a statement, read it aloud. Talk with a partner about why this is a generalization.

- Think about people, places, or objects in your reading and ask a partner if he or she can make a generalization about them, using key words such as *all, most, many,* or *none.*

- What kinds of generalizations have you heard before about something? Discuss with a partner or small group.

Do It!

- Use a graphic organizer such as the one below to help you make generalizations. Ask yourself if these statements can be supported by facts.

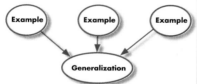

- With permission, collect related items around the classroom. Sketch the items and write 1-3 generalizations about them.

- Carry a notebook with you. Look for generalizations you can make about certain foods, games, plants, and so on.

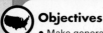

Objectives
- Make generalizations about a text.
- Analyze generalizations in text.

Skill

Strategy

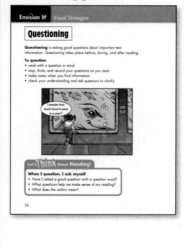

Comprehension Skill

Generalize

- Sometimes authors write broad statements that apply to many examples. These statements are called generalizations. Often, clue words such as *most, all, sometimes, always,* and *never* identify generalizations.

- Generalizations supported by facts and logic are called valid generalizations. Faulty generalizations are not supported by facts and logic.

- Generalizations should always be supported with facts from the text or from your knowledge of the world.

- Use a graphic organizer like the one below to help you generalize as you read "Ashley Helps Out."

Comprehension Strategy

Questioning

Active readers ask questions while they read. This can help them understand and evaluate the text, make predictions, and determine the author's purpose. Questioning is also useful when deciding whether or not an author's generalizations are valid or faulty. To evaluate generalizations, ask "Is this statement accurate?" or "Do facts support this statement?"

Ashley Helps Out

"I'll get it, Mom," said Ashley. She walked quickly to the buzzer and pressed it so her friend Karina could enter. Ashley loved living in the apartment with her mother, but who wouldn't? Apartments are always better to live in than houses because you don't have to trim the hedges, and they are always luxurious inside.

"Mom, Karina and I are going to the shelter now, okay?"

"Okay, baby," said a groggy voice from the back bedroom. Ashley's mother usually worked nights and had to sleep during the day.

At the homeless shelter, the girls volunteered to help serve dinner. Although the food wasn't very tasty (it never is at homeless shelters), Ashley dispensed the food with a smile and an encouraging word. Several hours later, the girls finished up and returned to the apartment.

"Mom, we're home," Ashley called as they entered. She and Karina fixed tuna sandwiches and a Greek salad to surprise Ashley's mom.

"Aw, sweetie, you're too much!" she said when she walked into the kitchen.

Strategy Asking questions before you read can help you predict what a story might be about. What questions come to mind from the title alone? Are they answered as you read?

Skill How can you determine if the author's generalization about apartments is valid or faulty?

Skill Is the generalization about food at homeless shelters valid or faulty? Why do you think so?

Your Turn!

⏸ **Need a Review?**
See *Envision It!* Skills and Strategies for additional help.

▶ **Ready to Try It?**
Use what you've learned about generalizing and questioning as you read other text.

Objectives

• Make generalizations about a text and use evidence from the text to support understanding.

Comprehension Skill

🎯 Generalize

• A generalization is a broad statement or rule that applies to many examples.

• Sometimes when you read, you can generalize. When you are given ideas about several things or people and you can make a statement that applies to all of them, you are generalizing.

• Valid generalizations are supported by examples, facts, or good logic. Invalid generalizations are not supported.

• Use a graphic organizer like the one below to make a generalization about "Tall-Tale Town."

Envision It! | Skill Strategy

Skill

Strategy

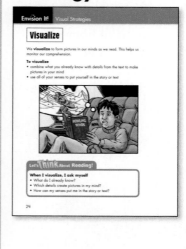

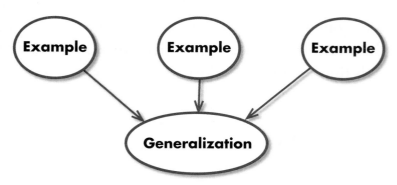

Comprehension Strategy

🎯 Visualize

Good readers visualize, or create mental images, to make sense of what they read. They picture themselves seeing, hearing, feeling, tasting, or smelling things or events in a text. Visualizing is a good way to understand the characters, setting, and events of a story.

Tall-Tale Town

Rahim was the new kid in town. One day he ventured out, looking to shoot some hoops and make some friends in the process.

"Hi," he said, as he approached a boy mowing the lawn. "Like to play basketball?"

Strategy
Visualize the boy mowing the lawn. What do you see, hear, and smell?

"Sure, just yesterday I was shooting some hoops at the playground and made 551 free throws in a row," the boy said.

"That's astounding!" exclaimed Rahim.

"Yeah, but I can't play now. I have to finish mowing the lawn. Maybe later."

Rahim continued on until he came to a boy washing the family car. "Like to play basketball?" he asked.

"Love to. I scored 242 points in a game once. Would have scored more, but my coach took me out for the second half. My knee is bothering me now. Maybe some other time."

Skill What can you generalize from how the second boy responds? Explain.

Rahim was speechless. "Like to play basketball?" he asked a third boy, a little hesitantly.

"Nope. Soccer's my game. Last week I blocked 863 shots on goal. We won the game, 1–0."

Rahim slowly wandered home.

"How'd it go, honey?" his mother inquired as he entered the back door. "Do you think you'll like it here?"

Rahim paused. "Yeah. Who wouldn't? We just moved to the greatest, smartest, most talented town in the world!"

Skill What generalization might be suggested about the people in the town?

Your Turn!

 Need a Review?
See *Envision It!* Skills and Strategies for additional help.

 Ready to Try It?
Use what you've learned about generalizing and visualizing as you read other text.

Envision It! | Skill Strategy

Skill

Strategy

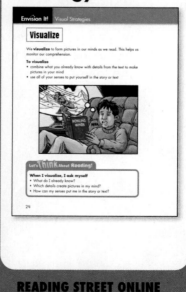

READING STREET ONLINE
ENVISION IT! ANIMATIONS
www.ReadingStreet.com

Comprehension Skill

Generalize

- A generalization is a broad statement that applies to many examples. Authors sometimes make generalizations to get across a message about a group of things or people.

- A generalization is often signaled by clue words such as *most, all, always,* or *never*.

- A generalization can be either valid or faulty. Valid generalizations are supported by examples, facts, or sound logic. Invalid generalizations cannot be supported.

- Use a graphic organizer like the one below to make a generalization about A. Philip Randolph in "Traveling Men."

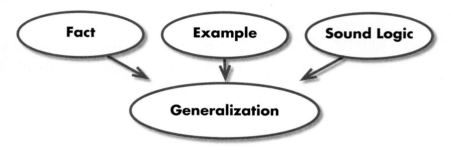

Comprehension Strategy

Visualize

Good readers look for sensory details to create pictures in their minds as they read. The sights, sounds, and smells described by an author help you to visualize what you are reading. As you read, think about the impact that sensory details and imagery have on the selection.

Traveling Men

Soon after the Civil War, two important events happened: slaves were freed, and the first intercontinental railroad was finished.

With the new, longer train trips, passengers needed a comfortable place to sleep on the train. Chicago businessman George Pullman claimed that his new sleeping cars offer luxury and service at affordable prices. Pullman hired former slaves, who did an excellent job working as porters on these luxury sleeping cars.

It was work the former slaves were glad to get. It gave them a steady job and respect in the neighborhood, where they were known as "traveling men."

However, their jobs were far from fair. Hours were long, pay was low, and porters could be fired for no reason. As time progressed, younger porters began to see that they deserved much better treatment. However, the Pullman company refused to make changes.

Because of the refusal, the porters formed a union in 1925 called the Brotherhood of Sleeping Car Porters, led by A. Philip Randolph. It took twelve long years of struggle, but the union finally won better pay and working conditions. And Randolph became a hero of the modern Civil Rights movement.

Skill The Emancipation Proclamation was signed in 1863. The Civil War ended in 1865. The railroad was completed in 1869. What generalization about the United States can you make from these examples?

Strategy How can visualizing help you understand what it was like to work as a sleeping-car porter? Which words and phrases help you?

Skill Would it be a valid generalization to say that all porters wanted to join a union and fight for better treatment and wages? Explain your thinking.

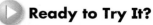

Your Turn!

❚❚ Need a Review? See *Envision It!* Skills and Strategies for additional help.

▶ Ready to Try It? Use what you've learned about generalizing and visualizing as you read other text.

Graphic Sources

A graphic source shows information in a way that the reader can see.

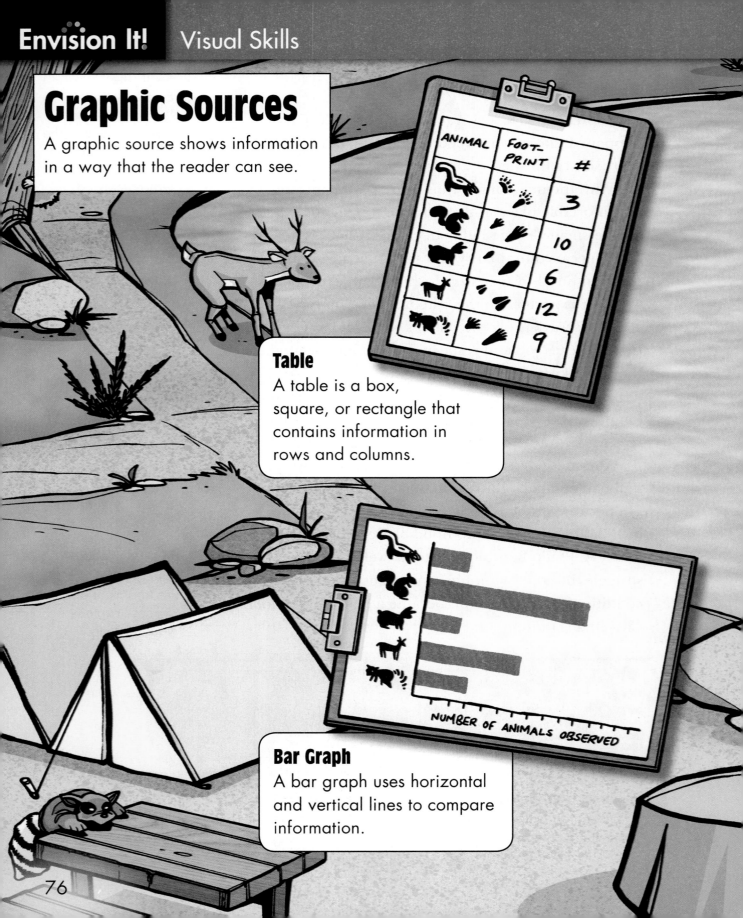

Table
A table is a box, square, or rectangle that contains information in rows and columns.

Bar Graph
A bar graph uses horizontal and vertical lines to compare information.

LAKE

N
W · E
S

CAMPSITE

Map
A map is a drawing of a place that shows where something is or where something happened.

HOW TO MAKE A

HANGER
OR
WIRE

BEND
THE
WIRE
TO MAKE A HOLDER AND
NAIL TO A FENCE

RAIN GAUGE

SCALE IN INCHES
INSIDE OF CAN

SMOOTH-SIDED CONTAINER
FITS IN HOLDER

Diagram
A diagram is a drawing, usually with parts that are labeled.

How to Use Graphic Sources

Graphic sources include charts, tables, graphs, maps, illustrations, and photographs. These features can help you see and understand information as well as predict what the reading will be about.

See It!

- Look at pages 76–77. What do you notice? What do the images and text tell you about how graphic sources make information easier to understand? Explain.

- During reading, scan the text for graphic sources that can help you understand the topic. These items usually reveal and tell more about the main ideas of a text.

- Pick a graphic source in your reading to examine in depth. What kind of information does it show? Is it easy to understand? Why might this information be important? Explain.

Say It!

- Pause in your reading when you come across graphic sources. Review the graphic source, then explain the information aloud with a partner.

- Sometimes it's hard to follow a text when you're not sure when to look at the graphic sources. Practice looking over them beforehand to prepare for reading the text.

- While reading and examining graphic sources, ask yourself or a partner, "What is the purpose of this graphic? Why would the author choose to include it?"

Do It!

- Make a chart such as the one below to use while reading.

Type of Graphic Source	What It Shows	How It Helps You Understand Information

- Create your own graphic source to go with something you've written or read. Be sure your graphic sources are properly labeled and relate to, or tell more about, your topic.

- Write a paragraph that tells about your favorite place. Include a graphic source with your paragraph, such as a labeled illustration of the place or a map of how to get there.

Objectives

• Use graphics and text features to gain an overview and to locate information in the text.

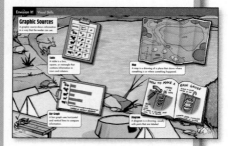

Skill

Strategy

Comprehension Skill

Graphic Sources

• Graphic sources such as maps, photographs, and time lines show information visually.

• As you read, compare information in a graphic source with information in the text.

• Use a Venn diagram like the one below to organize details about two very different groups of early Native American people.

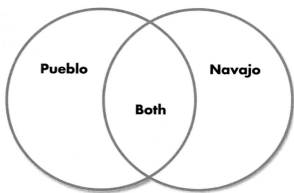

Comprehension Strategy

Text Structure

Good readers use the structure of an article to help them understand what they read. Before reading, preview the selection. Look at the title, headings, and captions to get an idea of what the selection will be about and how it is organized. Headings sometimes outline an article.

In One Place or On the Move

Group of Early People	Pueblo	Navajo
Way of Life	permanent settlements	nomadic
How They Got Food	farmed, raised turkeys, hunted, gathered	hunted, gathered
Foods	turkey, corn, squash, beans, sunflower seeds, game, wild plants	deer, elk, rabbits, birds, snakes, wild plants such as mesquite and cactus
Homes	permanent buildings, like apartments	temporary huts with covered poles

Skill Based on this graphic source, what do you think this article will be about?

Skill Use the chart to answer this question: How did the Navajo get their food?

Very early Native Americans in the Southwest lived in two different ways. Some, like the Pueblo, lived in one place. Others, like the Navajo, were nomadic and moved from place to place.

Different Lifestyles

Strategy What will this section be about? How can you tell?

Pueblo people lived in connected buildings made of stone or adobe brick. The buildings were something like apartments. They could be as high as five levels. The Pueblo also built special buildings where people gathered for meetings and ceremonies.

Nomadic people, such as the Navajo, would settle in one spot for a time. There they built huts with frames made of logs and poles. The frames were covered with mud, sod, and bark. When the Navajo moved on, they left their huts and built new ones in the next place.

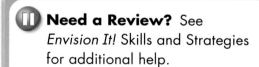
Your Turn!

 Need a Review? See *Envision It!* Skills and Strategies for additional help.

▶ **Ready to Try It?**
Use what you've learned about graphic sources and text structure as you read other text.

Objectives
• Summarize the main idea and supporting details in a text.
• Interpret information in maps, charts, illustrations, time lines, and so on.

Envision It! | Skill Strategy

Skill

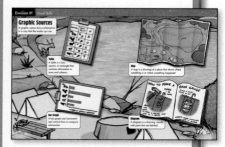

Strategy

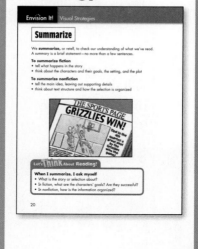

Comprehension Skill

Graphic Sources

• Graphic sources such as maps, charts, diagrams, pictures, and schedules give information visually.

• Graphic sources are often used to summarize complex information.

• Use a graphic source like the two-column chart below with the map on the next page to make better sense of the information you will read in "The Land of Egypt."

Rainfall in Egypt

Location	Rainfall as Inches per Year
Alexandria	7
Northern Sinai	5
Cairo	1
Aswan	1/10

Comprehension Strategy

Summarize

Summarizing helps you determine which information in an article is the most important. Summaries state only the important ideas and do not include minor details. A summary also can be in the form of a chart, graph, time line, or some other graphic aid, because the key information is put into the graphic with as few words as possible.

The Land of Egypt

The Nile The Nile River is the most important body of water in Egypt. Aside from being the main source of fresh water, this mighty river divides Egypt into two sections, the Western and Eastern Deserts. A third area, the Sinai, is also a desert.

Mountains Egypt is not a completely flat country. There are mountains along the coast of the Red Sea. The highest of these rises 7,175 feet. The Sinai holds Egypt's highest mountain, Mount Catherine, which has an elevation of 8,668 feet.

Climate Egypt is a very sunny place. It averages 12 hours of sunshine per day in the summer and about 10 hours in the winter. Winters are usually cool, with temperatures around 65°F. In summer, the highs range from 91°F in Cairo to 106°F in Aswan. Long winter cold spells and summer heat waves are not uncommon.

Precipitation On average, Egypt receives very little rain. Most of the rain comes during the winter months. However, the amount varies from place to place. The farther south you go in Egypt, the less it rains.

Strategy What is the most important information you read in this paragraph? Summarize this first paragraph in one sentence.

Skill How does the map below help you better understand the information in this paragraph?

Skill How does the "Rainfall in Egypt" graphic on the previous page help you understand the information presented in this article?

MEDITERRANEAN SEA
ISRAEL
Mount Catherine
Alexandria
N
SINAI
Cairo
JORDAN
W E
SAUDI ARABIA
S
EGYPT
Nile River
RED SEA
Aswan

Your Turn!

⏸ **Need a Review?** See *Envision It!* Skills and Strategies for additional help.

▶ **Ready to Try It?** Use what you've learned about graphic sources and summarizing as you read other text.

Objectives
• Use text features and graphics to gain an overview and to locate information in the text. • Interpret information in maps, charts, illustrations, graphs, time lines, tables, and diagrams.

Envision It! | Skill Strategy

Skill

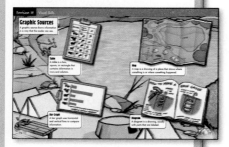

Strategy

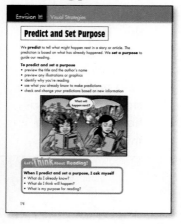

Comprehension Skill

Graphic Sources

- Graphic sources include maps, charts, diagrams, and other visual presentations of information.

- While reading, study the information in the graphic sources and ask: What does this information tell me about this topic? How does this graphic connect to what I'm reading in the text?

- A graphic organizer like the one below can help to organize ideas based on "Greece: Land and Climate." This chart suggests the kind of clothing that ancient Greeks might have worn year-round.

Greek Clothing		
Clothing type	**Indoor**	**Outdoor**
Regular clothing	tunic	tunic
Heavier clothing		cloak
On feet	shoeless	sandals
On head	hatless	veil or hat

Comprehension Strategy

Predict and Set Purpose

Active readers try to predict what they will learn when they read a nonfiction text. Previewing an article is a good way to predict what you will be reading and to establish a purpose for reading it. Establishing a purpose for reading something can help you comprehend it better.

GREECE: Land and Climate

Greece is a country in Europe. It is made up of a mainland and more than 2,000 islands that have a total area of 50,949 square miles. While Greece is known as a rocky place with many mountains, it also has some level ground.

The Land Because Greece touches the Mediterranean, Ionian, and Aegean Seas, it has a great deal of coastline. In fact, there is only one small area in all of Greece that is farther than fifty miles from the coast.

Several mountain ranges run across the country, forming many narrow valleys. Some of the tallest mountains in Greece are Mt. Smolikas (8,652 feet), Mt. Orvilos (7,287 feet), and Mt. Parnassus (8,061 feet).

THE LAND OF GREECE

= mountains
= lowlands

The Climate Greece has a comfortable climate. Warm southern winds blow on Greece during the winter months. The average January temperature in Thessaloniki, in the north, is 43°F, while Athens, farther south, averages 50°F and Iraklion, even farther south, averages 54°F. In the summer it is dry and hot all over Greece. The normal July temperature is 80°F.

Strategy The title will help you predict what the selection is about. Read the title and then set a purpose for reading based on what you think the selection is about.

Skill Refer to the pie chart to choose the best answer.
a) Greece has more lowlands than mountains.
b) Most of Greece's land is mountainous.
c) Greeks like the mountains.

Skill Does the information in the pie chart relate to the information presented in this paragraph of the text? Why or why not?

Your Turn!

 Need a Review? See *Envision It!* Skills and Strategies for additional help.

Ready to Try It? Use what you've learned about graphic sources and predicting and setting a purpose as you read other text.

Literary Elements

A Day at the Beach

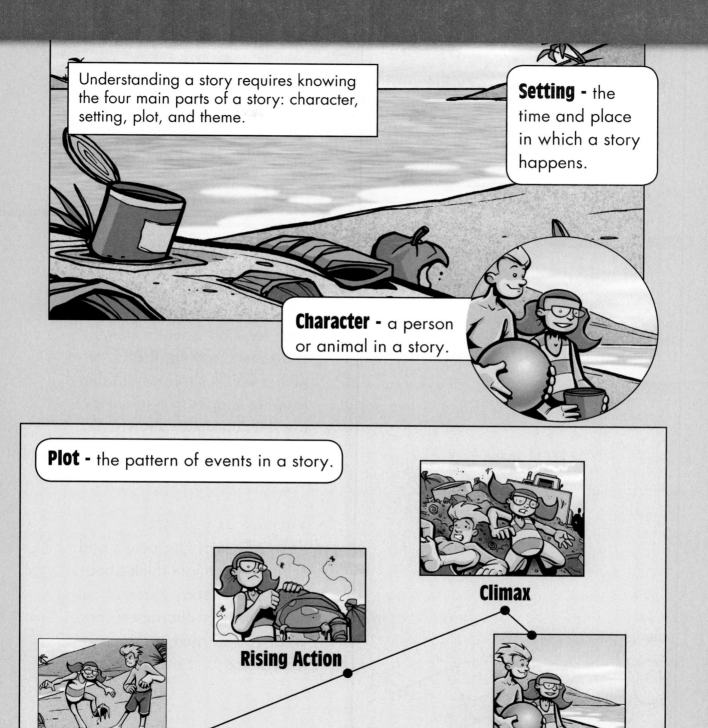

Understanding a story requires knowing the four main parts of a story: character, setting, plot, and theme.

Setting - the time and place in which a story happens.

Character - a person or animal in a story.

Plot - the pattern of events in a story.

Climax

Rising Action

Conflict

Solution

Theme - the big idea of a story.

How to Identify Literary Elements

Stories are made up of the following parts: character, setting, theme, and plot. Recognizing these literary elements will help you better understand the stories and books that you read.

See It!

- Look at pages 86–87. What do the pictures tell you about literary elements?

- Look for hints about a story's characters, setting, theme, or plot in the illustrations or other graphic images in a text. How are the characters shown? Do the images fit with the author's descriptions?

- Visualize as you read descriptions of characters and setting. You might think about what you already know about such places or characters, or what you've seen in movies or television.

Say It!

- Read aloud the text on pages 86–87. What do you learn about characters, setting, theme, and plot?

- Tell a partner about the characters, setting, theme, and plot of a book or movie you know well. If you are stuck on theme, think about what the most important ideas were in your own words.

- Each person in a group of four should pick a literary element to focus on (character, setting, plot, or theme) during reading. When finished reading, come back together as a group and talk about what you noticed.

Do It!

- After reading, make a list of important events that happened first, next, and last. What problems do the characters encounter? How were these problems resolved?

- What do you imagine the characters and setting of a story look like? Draw what you imagine. Include a caption.

- Make a graphic organizer like the one below, and fill in the details:

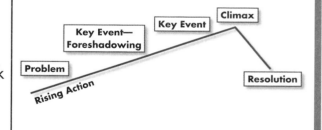

Key Event—Foreshadowing · Key Event · Climax · Problem · Rising Action · Resolution

 Need a Review? See *Envision It!* Skills and Strategies for additional help.

▶ **Ready to Try It?** Use what you've learned about setting and plot and visualizing as you read other text.

Envision It! | Skill Strategy

Skill

Strategy

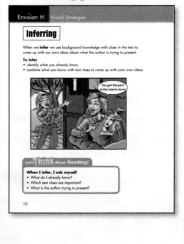

Comprehension Skill

Literary Elements: Setting and Plot

Comprehension Skill

Literary Elements: Character and Theme

- Characters are the people who take part in the events of the story.

- Theme is the main idea or central meaning of a piece of writing. The theme is often not stated. You can find it using evidence from the story as clues.

- Use a graphic organizer like the one below to identify characters and theme as you read "Linda and Val."

Characters	Val and Linda
Theme	
First clue	Linda does not want to work with Val because of her physical challenge.
Second clue	When Val's fingers will not open, the girls cooperate as Linda pries Val's hand open.
Third clue	Linda decides to be friends with Val and that she likes working with her.

Comprehension Strategy

Inferring

Authors do not always directly tell readers everything about the characters, events, and theme in a story. Sometimes you need to infer, or figure out, what is not stated directly.

LINDA AND VAL

"Today we'll weigh objects. For homework, you'll make a graph of the weights," Mr. Daniels said. "Linda, you work with Val."

Linda's eyes widened in disbelief. "Val?" Linda said. Val had joined the class just last week. She had cerebral palsy.

Linda looked at Val, who was attempting to stand up. Her arms and legs shook. Linda rolled her eyes. Val slowly wobbled over and said, "Hi, Linda." Linda did not reply.

Once Val sat down, Linda asked, "Have you ever weighed an object?"

"Sure, even shaky old me," Val joked. The humorous reply surprised Linda, and she relaxed a little.

Val tried to place a weight on the scale, but her hand stayed closed. Then her clenched fist began to shake. "Could you pry that open for me?" Val asked. Linda slowly peeled Val's fingers back until the weight dropped. "Nice job," Val said, smiling. "You didn't even need a crowbar." Linda smiled. "Do you want me to put the next weight on?" she asked.

"Sure, this time I might never let go!" Val quipped. Both girls laughed and continued working. At the end of the class, Val asked, "Do you want to come over to my home after school? We could work on the graph together."

Linda didn't even hesitate. "Sure."

Skill Remember that you can learn about a character by the way he or she acts. What does Linda's facial expression tell you about her?

Skill Linda has begun to change her actions and words toward Val. What does this tell you about Val's character?

Strategy Linda and Val may become friends after this experience. What do you think caused this to happen?

Your Turn!

❚❚ Need a Review? See *Envision It!* Skills and Strategies for additional help.

▶ Ready to Try It? Use what you've learned about literary elements and inferring as you read other text.

93

Envision It! | Skill Strategy

Skill

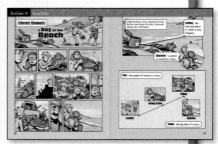

Strategy

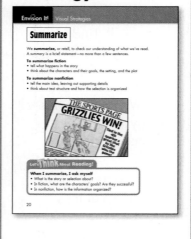

Comprehension Skill

Literary Elements: Plot and Theme

• Recognizing literary elements—plot, characters, setting, theme—will help you better understand the stories and books that you read.

• The plot includes (1) a *problem* or *goal;* (2) *rising action,* or events when a character tries to solve the problem or meet the goal; (3) a *climax,* when the character meets the problem or goal head-on; and (4) a *resolution,* or outcome.

• The theme is the main idea of a story.

• Make a graphic organizer like the one below to help you chart the plot in "Jarrett's Journal."

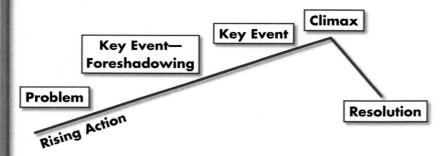

Comprehension Strategy

Summarize

Good readers can better understand a story by summarizing, or briefly stating in their own words, the story's plot and theme. When you summarize a story, concentrate on the main events rather than the details.

JARRETT'S JOURNAL

April 16—It's a very relaxing evening—the very opposite of today! Today I was going to host a dinner at 6 o'clock in my new apartment for my grandparents, parents, and 12-year-old brother, Billy. <u>Was going to</u> is the operative phrase.

This morning I rolled over in bed and glanced at the clock. It was noon! I was so exhausted from moving that I'd neglected to set my alarm. I darted out of bed and started sweeping and scrubbing and piling boxes and stuff that was lying around into closets and my dresser drawers.

Then I dashed out to the supermarket. When I got back, I rinsed the chicken I'd just bought, plopped it into a pan, poured a gourmet sauce over it, and stuck it in the oven.

Next I got the potatoes and salad ready and set the table. Finally I readied myself, showering and putting on a clean pair of jeans. Six o'clock—the security buzzer rang.

With my family peering over my shoulder, I opened the oven and voila! a pink, flabby, RAW chicken. I'd forgotten to turn on the oven!

"Nice going," my brother said with a smirk. "Now what are we going to eat?"

It's a good thing there's an outstanding pizza parlor just down the block.

Skill What is the problem in this story?

Skill What is the climax? What is the resolution?

Strategy Use the main events of the story to summarize.

Your Turn!

Need a Review? See *Envision It!* Skills and Strategies for additional help.

Ready to Try It? Use what you've learned about plot and theme and summarizing as you read other text.

Main Idea and Details

Main idea is the most important idea about a topic. For example, it takes a lot of people to put on a big rock concert.

Details are smaller pieces of information that support the main idea. Musicians, technicians, and fans are all part of the rock concert experience.

How to Identify Main Idea and Details

The main idea is the most important idea. Details are the pieces of information that tell more about—or help explain—this main idea.

See It!

- Look at page 96. What details are pictured? What do you think is the main idea? Why? How do the picture's details help you understand the main idea?

- Use illustrations, graphs, and other images to help you figure out the main idea of your reading. What information do you get from the images? How does this help you tell the main idea?

- Look at the first paragraph or paragraphs of a text. Most often, the author states the main idea here.

Say It!

- With a partner, state the main idea. Each of you should come up with at least one example from the reading that supports, or proves, this statement. If you cannot, you may have not correctly identified the main idea.

- To check if you have correctly identified the main idea, tell it to a partner after reading. Ask him or her: "Does my main idea make sense? Does it cover all the important details?"

- Sometimes slowing down and reading aloud can help you pick up on important supporting details.

Do It!

- Use a web like the one below:

- What detail does not support this main idea? *A good night's sleep is important before taking a test.*
a) It's hard to concentrate when you are tired.
b) Setting an alarm helps you get ready on time.
c) Short-term memory can be affected by lack of sleep.

- Write why you like a movie or book. Circle the main idea and underline the supporting details.

97

Objectives
- Summarize the main idea and supporting details in a text.
- Monitor and clarify comprehension by rereading.

Envision It! | Skill Strategy

Skill

Strategy

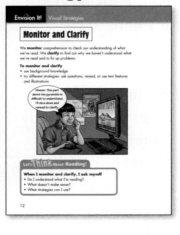

Comprehension Skill

🎯 Main Idea and Details

- To find the topic of a paragraph or selection, ask yourself, "What is this text about?"

- To find the main idea, ask yourself, "What is the most important idea about the topic?" Often it is in the first sentence of a key paragraph.

- Once you find the main idea, look for supporting details that explain or tell about the main idea.

- As you read "The Telescope," use two graphic organizers like the one below, one for "Optical Telescopes" and the other for "Radio Telescopes," to help you determine the main idea and supporting details about each telescope.

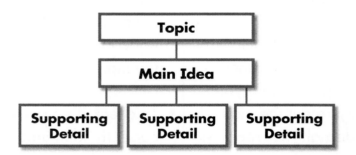

Comprehension Strategy

🎯 Monitor and Clarify

When you are reading, it's important to know when you understand something and when you don't. If you are confused, you can use text features such as headings to clarify information. You can also look back and reread, either silently or aloud.

The Telescope

For thousands of years humans studied the sky using only their eyes. Today, however, astronomers have a much more powerful tool to use: the telescope. There are two kinds of telescopes: optical and radio.

Strategy Text features such as headings can help you find topics. What is the topic of this paragraph?

Optical Telescopes

Optical telescopes work by collecting light. The larger the aperture, or opening, of the telescope, the more powerful it is. The largest optical telescope in the world is in Russia. It has an opening 236 inches wide. Most of the world's large, powerful optical telescopes are in buildings called observatories. These are usually high on mountains, away from cities and lights. Some, such as the Hubble Space Telescope, are in space.

Skill Which of the following sentences best states the main idea of the section "Optical Telescopes"?
a) Optical telescopes work by collecting light.
b) The largest optical telescope is in Russia.
c) Most large optical telescopes are in observatories.

Radio Telescopes

Radio telescopes collect long energy waves from far-away objects in space through a "dish," a curved object that looks like a bowl. The world's largest radio telescope, in Germany, is almost 300 feet wide! The most powerful radio telescope, though, is in New Mexico. Scientists use it to study the solar system and other galaxies.

Skill What is the main idea of the section "Radio Telescopes"?

Without telescopes, we would know very little about the amazing objects in the sky.

Your Turn!

 Need a Review? See *Envision It!* Skills and Strategies for additional help.

Ready to Try It? Use what you've learned about main idea and details and monitoring and clarifying as you read other text.

Objectives
• Identify the main idea and supporting details in a text.
• Explore and come to conclusions about informative writing, and show proof from the text to support your research.

Envision It! | Skill Strategy

Skill

Strategy

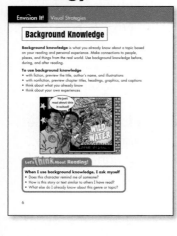

Comprehension Skill

Main Idea and Details

• The topic of a selection can usually be stated in a few words.

• The main idea is the most important idea about the topic. It is often stated at or near the beginning of a selection.

• Supporting details tell more about the main idea.

• As you read, look for details that link back to the main idea.

• Use a graphic organizer like the one below as you read "Artifacts."

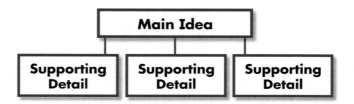

Comprehension Strategy

Background Knowledge

Background knowledge is what you already know about a topic, either on your own or from your reading. Good readers connect that knowledge to what they read in order to understand better and remember more.

ARTIFACTS

The continent of Asia has some of the oldest civilizations on Earth. Evidence of how early people in that area lived is studied by archaeologists. Archaeologists are scientists who study past human cultures. They look at artifacts that have been uncovered.

What is an artifact? Any object made by a human and then later discovered by an archaeologist is called an artifact. Artifacts tell scientists about the culture of an ancient civilization. These artifacts are often buried for centuries and have to be carefully excavated during a dig.

How are artifacts found? In order not to harm artifacts, members of an excavation team follow certain procedures. They might first use special radar to look below ground. Then special instruments help move away layers of soil. All of the results must be documented. The entire process often takes years, as was the case with the Terracotta army, in China.

What do artifacts tell? Some artifacts have been able to tell archaeologists what people in an ancient civilization ate or what they did for entertainment. Most often artifacts reveal the materials, skills, and technology that ancient people used.

Strategy Read the title and bold headings. What are some things you already know about artifacts?

Skill What is the main idea of this section?

Skill What supporting detail from this paragraph could you add to your graphic organizer?

Your Turn!

⏸ **Need a Review?** See *Envision It!* Skills and Strategies for additional help.

▶ **Ready to Try It?** Use what you've learned about main idea and details and background knowledge as you read other text.

101

Objectives
- Summarize the main ideas and supporting details in a text.
- Use text features and graphics to gain an overview and locate information.

Envision It! | Skill Strategy

Skill

Strategy

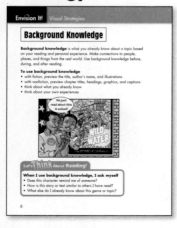

Comprehension Skill

Main Idea and Details

- The main idea is the most important idea about a topic. Details are less important pieces of information that tell more about the main idea.

- Sometimes an author states the main idea of a paragraph or an entire article in a single sentence at the beginning or the end or, rarely, in the middle of the writing.

- The topic of a paragraph can usually be stated in a word or two. Look to the first sentence to find out what the paragraph will be about.

- Use a graphic organizer like the one below to identify the main idea and supporting details of "Metals."

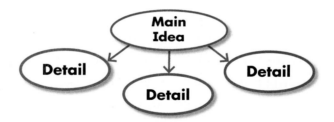

Comprehension Strategy

Background Knowledge

Good readers use what they already know to understand what they are reading. As you read about metals, think about what you already know about these substances. Making these connections will help you become a more active reader.

METALS

WHAT ARE METALS? Some substances, such as gold, iron, aluminum, and silver, are called metals. They are good conductors, meaning that it is easy for heat or electricity to flow through them. Metals are also malleable, which means they can be shaped and made flat.

ARE THERE MANY METALS? There are many different metals on Earth. In fact, three-fourths of all of the chemical substances humans know about are metals. Many, such as iron, are found in the Earth's crust.

WHAT TYPES OF METALS ARE THERE? Metals are grouped in three categories based on their characteristics. There are alkali metals, alkaline-earth metals, and transition metals. Alkali metals, such as sodium, dissolve in water. The molecules in these metals often join with other elements to form new substances. Alkaline-earth metals also dissolve in water, and the new substances they form are often found in nature. Calcium, which is found in your bones, is an alkaline-earth metal. Transition metals are the largest group of metals. Most metals that are used in everyday life, such as copper and iron, are transition metals. These metals are hard, strong, and shiny.

Strategy Consider what you already know about metals as you read this paragraph. What metals have you seen? What did they look like? What did they feel like?

Skill The topic of this paragraph is the quantity of metals. What is the main idea of the paragraph?

Skill What is the main idea of this paragraph? What is one detail about each kind of metal?

Your Turn!

Need a Review? See *Envision It!* Skills and Strategies for additional help.

Ready to Try It? Use what you've learned about main idea and details and background knowledge as you read other text.

Sequence

Sequence refers to the order that events happen.
We use sequence when we list the steps in a process.

How to Identify Sequence

The sequence is the order in which events take place, from first to last.

See It!

- Does the story have illustrations or other images? If so, do they give you any clues about what happens first, next, and last?

- Look at page 104. What do you see happening first, next, and last? Tell the sequence to a partner.

- Look for clue words, such as *first, next, then,* or *after.* They will help tell you the order of a story. *While* and *at the same time* hint that events are occurring at the same time. If a writer does not use clue words, try to picture the sequence in your mind.

Say It!

- Take turns telling a partner what happens first, next, and last in the story.

- Retell what has been read by asking, "What have I just read?" Summarize the events. Do this when you feel confused or haven't read the story for a few days—it will help you identify sequence.

- Because some authors tell a story out of sequence, ask a classmate to paraphrase, or tell in his or her own words, what happened in the story from beginning to end. How does this help you tell the order of events of the story?

Do It!

- Draw images that match the story's events. Be sure to put your illustrations in order of first, next, and last.

- Make a sequence diagram or a time line to help you keep track of important events in the story.

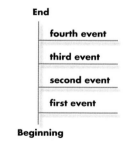

- In groups, perform different parts of the story out of order. Groups then should perform the story in order from beginning to end.

Objectives
● Analyze how the organization of a text, such as sequential order, affects the ways ideas are related.
● Connect background knowledge to text to strengthen comprehension.

Envision It! | Skill Strategy

Skill

Strategy

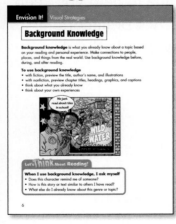

Comprehension Skill

Sequence

- Sequence is the order of events in a story. Clue words such as *first, next, then,* and *finally* often indicate sequence.

- If events happen at the same time, look for clue words such as *while* and *during.*

- Use a graphic organizer like the one below to keep track of the sequence of events in "Incident at the Street Fair."

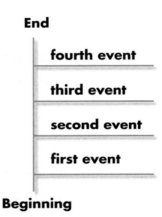

End

fourth event

third event

second event

first event

Beginning

Comprehension Strategy

Background Knowledge

Background knowledge is what you already know about a topic from your reading or from your real-life experience. Use background knowledge before, during, and after reading to monitor your comprehension.

Incident at the Street Fair

One Saturday Caleb, his sister Mandy, and their father rode the train downtown to the Garfield Street Festival. The street fair was packed with people!

First they treated themselves to some barbecued chicken and corn at a food booth and listened to a live salsa band entertaining the crowd from the main stage. While his father surveyed his festival map, Caleb gazed up at the glistening skyline, tilting his head w-a-a-a-y back.

"Dad, look at that awesome skyscraper," Caleb said, but there was no reply. Caleb anxiously glanced all around, but he didn't see a single familiar face.

Wide-eyed, Caleb wandered around, looking for his family in all directions. At one point he was sure he saw his father—the shirt was the same. But when Caleb tapped on the shirt and the person wearing it turned around, all Caleb saw was an old man eating a sloppy sandwich with barbecue sauce all over his face. Caleb was getting nervous.

The crowd swelled larger, and people bumped and jostled him. A rock band was now playing ear-blasting music. Then suddenly he saw Mandy and, a moment later, his father's face. It held a strange mixture of anger and relief.

Skill Which of the following events took place at the same time Caleb was looking at the skyline?
a) He began to walk around.
b) His father looked at a map.
c) He ate chicken and corn.

Strategy Have you ever been separated from your family in a crowd? How would that experience help you understand how Caleb is feeling at this point?

Skill What is the last event in the story?

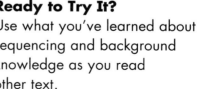

Your Turn!

Need a Review? See *Envision It!* Skills and Strategies for additional help.

Ready to Try It?
Use what you've learned about sequencing and background knowledge as you read other text.

Skill

Strategy

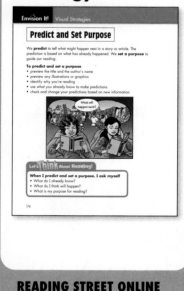

READING STREET ONLINE
ENVISION IT! ANIMATIONS
www.ReadingStreet.com

Comprehension Skill

Sequence

- Sequence is the order in which events take place, from first to last.

- The time of day and clue words such as *before* and *after* or *first, next, then,* and *finally* can help you determine sequence.

- Sequence is used to organize both fiction and nonfiction writing.

- Use a graphic organizer like the one below to establish a time line that shows the sequence of events in "Slow Down!"

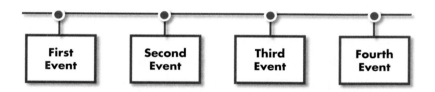

| First Event | Second Event | Third Event | Fourth Event |

Comprehension Strategy

Predict and Set Purpose

Before reading, good readers predict what will happen or what they will learn and then establish a purpose for reading. Setting a purpose can help you understand a text. When you've finished reading, look back to see if your predictions were accurate.

Slow Down!

Thunder boomed. Glen and Felix huddled under an overhanging rock, but Dave, standing, said, "Let's keep going."

"No way," Felix said, as it thundered and lightning flashed. Glen nodded. Dave scowled.

Once the storm passed, the three young men resumed their hike. They walked through a small woods, then out across a meadow where a herd of elk was grazing. An hour later the three approached a river. It was wide and fast. Glen and Felix walked along the bank to find a safer place to cross, where the water was shallower and the current not so strong. Dave stopped.

"C'mon already!" Dave yelled. Felix and Glen didn't reply; it was crazy to even consider crossing there. A minute later Felix glanced back and saw Dave striding into the deep, churning water. Felix rushed down the bank, but the current was already hurtling Dave downstream.

"The rope!" Felix yelled to Glen, who quickly pulled it out of his pack. Glen threw one end of the rope to Dave and dragged him to shore.

"I could've made it," Dave said, standing on shore. Felix and Glen just rolled their eyes.

Skill What phrase at the beginning of this paragraph is a clue to sequence? What other clue words and phrases are in this paragraph?

Strategy Think of how Dave acted during the storm. What do you predict he will do next?

Skill What do you think the last important event should be on your time line of this story?

Your Turn!

⏸ **Need a Review?** See *Envision It!* Skills and Strategies for additional help.

▶ **Ready to Try It?** Use what you've learned about sequencing and predicting and setting a purpose as you read other text.

Objectives
● Analyze how the organization of a text, such as sequential order, affects the way ideas are related.
● Understand how to use the strategy of monitor and clarify.

Envision It! | Skill Strategy

Skill

Strategy

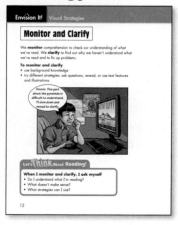

READING STREET ONLINE
ENVISION IT! ANIMATIONS
www.ReadingStreet.com

Comprehension Skill

Sequence

- Sequence refers to the order of events or the steps in a process.

- Dates, times, and clue words such as *first, next, then,* and *last* can help you determine sequence.

- Sometimes a text will present events out of order. In that case, you can read on, review, or reread in order to learn the correct sequence.

- Use a graphic organizer like the one below to show the sequence of important events in "Weather Watch."

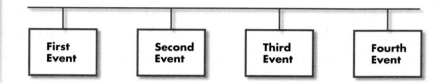

| **First Event** | **Second Event** | **Third Event** | **Fourth Event** |

Comprehension Strategy

Monitor and Clarify

One strategy good readers use to get back on track when they are confused is to keep reading. Confusion is often cleared up when you've read the entire section or text. If you are still confused, go back to the confusing section and see if it helps to reread the text.

WEATHER WATCH

Early on Saturday morning, August 10, we listened closely to the weather forecast. A hurricane brewed fiercely in the Gulf, and we wanted to know if we might have to evacuate. Weather watches stated that we should pay careful attention but that there was no need to leave our home at that point.

By that night, the hurricane had not changed direction. Mom said that we should buy canned goods, water, and batteries for our flashlights and radios and then hunker down at home and continue to listen to the weather. We headed for the grocery store.

On Sunday afternoon, August 11, the hurricane had changed course just slightly, but we weren't in the clear yet. We loaded our supplies in a big box and put them near the back door so we could quickly put them into the car, if necessary. Then we went to fill our gas tank. We wanted to be ready to evacuate if the hurricane wobbled back our way.

Early Monday morning, we learned that the hurricane had veered away from land and we would not have to evacuate. We took the supplies out of the box near the back door, sighed a big sigh of relief, and headed out to see a movie.

Strategy If you do not understand what is happening with the weather, continue to read in order to clarify.

Skill How does this sentence help you figure out the sequence of events?

Skill What are clue words that help you determine the sequence of events? How do they help you?

Your Turn!

 Need a Review? See *Envision It!* Skills and Strategies for additional help.

▶ **Ready to Try It?** Use what you've learned about sequence and monitoring and clarifying as you read other text.

Let's Think About...

Vocabulary Skills and Strategies

Vocabulary skills and strategies are tools you use to help you figure out the meanings of words. Knowing the meanings of vocabulary will help you better understand what you read.

As you read, if you come to a word that you do not know,
- know when to use word parts to figure out its meaning.
- know when to use words in the surrounding text to figure out its meaning.
- know when to use a dictionary or glossary to figure out its meaning.

Ready to Try It?

 | Vocabulary

Related Words

Context Clues

Antonyms

Synonyms

Prefixes

Suffixes

Dictionary

Thesaurus

Multiple-Meaning Words

Base Words/Root Words

Word Origins: Roots

Related Words

Related words are words that all have the same base word.

invent

invention

inventor

Strategy for Related Words

1. Find the base word in your unfamiliar word.
2. Identify the meaning of the base word.
3. Guess the meaning of the unfamiliar word. Does it make sense in the sentence?
4. Use a dictionary to check your guess.

Context Clues

Context clues are the words and sentences found around an unknown word that may help you figure out a word's meaning.

My mother and I bought some delicious fruit today. We bought bananas, grapes, apples, and my favorite—kiwis!

Strategy for Context Clues

1. Look for clues in the words and phrases around the unknown word.
2. Take a guess at the word's meaning. Does it make sense in the sentence?
3. Use a dictionary to check your guess.

Objective
• Determine the meanings of unfamiliar words by using the context of the sentence.

corridors

groping

menacing

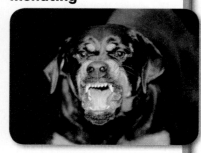

destination

mongrel

persisted

pleas

Vocabulary Strategy for
◎ Unfamiliar Words

Context Clues Sometimes you can use context clues—the words and sentences around an unfamiliar word—to help you figure out the meaning of the word.

1. Read the words and sentences around the unfamiliar word. The author may give you a definition of the word, examples, or a relationship that can help you predict the word's meaning.

2. If not, say what the sentence means in your own words.

3. Predict a meaning for the unfamiliar word.

4. Try your predicted meaning in the sentence. Does it make sense?

Read "The Traveler." Use context clues to help you figure out the meanings of any unfamiliar words you find.

Words to Write Reread "The Traveler." Imagine you find an animal that needs to be rescued, and write about how you would rescue it. Use words from the Words to Know list as you write.

The Traveler

The dog I found standing in the yard was a hungry-looking mongrel. He was put together like a puzzle of many different breeds. Every rib stuck out. He might have been lost or even abandoned. I knew he had belonged to someone, for he was not one bit menacing. He wagged his tail politely and lowered his head to be petted. This dog had manners, and someone had taught them to him.

The feel of his ribs made me wince. I made for the kitchen. While I was groping in the cupboard for some bread, I thought I saw a movement. Sure enough, he had started trotting down the road. I tore back to the yard like a sprinter, hollering after him. He was deaf to my pleas that he return. Instead, he persisted in moving off at a brisk pace. It was as if he had a destination set in his mind. How far did he have to go, and how would he survive?

In the years since then, I have often wondered with a twinge of regret whether that dog made it home. I cannot forget his faithful path through the dusty corridors of that lost summer.

Your Turn!

 Need a Review?
For help using context clues to determine the meanings of unfamiliar words, see page 115.

▶ **Ready to Try It?**
As you read other text, use context clues to help you figure out the meanings of unfamiliar words.

117

Objectives
• Determine the meanings of unfamiliar words by using context clues.

Envision It! | Words to Know

combustion

dingy

waft

negotiate

traversed

waning

Vocabulary Strategy for

Unfamiliar Words

Context Clues When you come across a word you do not know, use context clues—the words and sentences around the word—to figure out the meaning of the new word.

1. Reread the sentence in which the unfamiliar word appears. Look for a synonym, example, or other clue around the word that gives a clue to the word's meaning.

2. If you need more help, read the sentences around the sentence with the unknown word.

3. Stop and ask yourself, "What is this selection about?" The content itself may help you clarify the word's meaning.

4. Add up the clues you have found and predict the word's meaning. See if your meaning makes sense in the sentence.

Read "Lunar Love Affair." Look for context clues to determine meanings of unfamiliar words.

Words to Write Reread "Lunar Love Affair." Imagine you are traveling to the moon. Write a journal entry about your trip. Use words from the Words to Know list as you write.

Lunar Love Affair

The love affair of humans for all things lunar reaches far back into history. For many thousands of years, humans have watched the moon in the night sky. They saw it gradually waxing, or growing round, and then waning, or growing ever smaller, until only a sliver remained. It excited wonder and curiosity. No matter how dingy or ugly or hard life on Earth might be, the moon always glowed with a soft, pure light in the darkness. The perfume of blossoms might waft in the breeze, gently blowing faces turned up to gaze at the mysterious moon.

Then, not so long ago, people invented internal-combustion engines. By burning fuel in an enclosed space, they harnessed great power to drive vehicles, then airplanes, then jets. Before long, humans looked at the moon with a new question: Why not go there ourselves?

By 1969, astronauts had traversed outer space to go to the moon! Cameras showed us men in spacesuits taking great leaps across the rocky surface of the moon. It seemed the beginning of a new age. However, it seems that people have more plans than money for space travel. NASA, the U.S. agency responsible for space exploration, has to negotiate carefully for funding. Rather than return to the moon, humans have explored farther into space.

Your Turn!

Ⅱ Need a Review? For help using context clues to determine the meanings of unfamiliar words, see page 115.

▶ Ready to Try It? As you read other text, use context clues to help you determine the meanings of unfamiliar words.

Objectives
● Determine the meanings of unfamiliar words by using the context of the sentence and surrounding words.

Envision It! | Words to Know

insulated

isolation

provisions

conquer

destiny

expedition

navigator

verify

Vocabulary Strategy for
🎯 Unfamiliar Words

Context Clues When you come across a word that is unfamiliar, the author may have provided clues that can help you figure out its meaning. Look at the context, or the words and sentences around the unfamiliar word, for help.

Choose one of the Words to Know and follow these steps.

1. Reread the sentence in which the unfamiliar word appears.

2. Look for a specific clue in the words near the unfamiliar word.

3. If there isn't one, think about the overall meaning of the sentence. Does that give you a clue?

4. If you need more help, read the sentences near the unfamiliar word. They may contain clues or additional information that suggest the word's meaning.

5. Determine a meaning for the word based on any clues you have found. Try your meaning in the sentence. Does it make sense?

Read "Exploring the Unknown." Use context clues to help you figure out the meanings of any unfamiliar words.

Words to Write Reread "Exploring the Unknown." What frontier would you like to explore? Write about your expedition. Use as many words from the Words to Know list as you can.

Exploring the Unknown

There have always been people determined to conquer the unexplored corners of the world. Whether they have battled their way to the top of the Earth, the bottom of the ocean, or the silence of the moon, explorers feel it is their destiny to be the first.

They plan, organize, and outfit each expedition. To improve their odds of surviving, they take along food, clothing, transportation, and tools. They gather everything they think they will need to protect them from the cold or the heat and the extremes of nature. However, for all their provisions and planning, explorers are not insulated against the dangers of the unknown or of isolation.

The navigator may be able to tell explorers exactly where they stand. Yet he or she can never verify that the group will make it safely there and back. Think of a little knot of people standing on Mars sometime in the future. Will they have reached their goal?

Your Turn!

 Need a Review? For help using context clues to determine the meanings of unfamiliar words, see page 115.

▶ **Ready to Try It?**
As you read other text, use context clues to help you determine the meanings of unfamiliar words.

Objective

● Determine the meanings of unfamiliar words by using the context of the sentence.

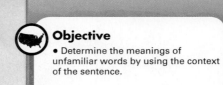

Envision It! | Words to Know

earthen

homesteaders

settlement

bondage

encounter

commissioned

Vocabulary Strategy for

🎯 Unfamiliar Words

Context Clues When you come across a word you do not know, check its context, or the words and sentences around the unfamiliar word. Often an author provides clues that suggest the word's meaning. When you encounter an unfamiliar word, follow these steps.

1. Reread the sentence in which the unfamiliar word appears. Look for a specific clue to the word's meaning.

2. Think about the overall meaning of the sentence.

3. Next read the sentences near the sentence with the unfamiliar word. They may contain enough information about the word and the subject to suggest the meaning of the unfamiliar word.

4. See if your meaning makes sense in the original sentence.

Read "Settling the West" on page 123. Use context clues to help you figure out the meanings of any unfamiliar words you may find.

Words to Write Reread "Settling the West." Study the photograph and write a description of it. Use words from the Words to Know list as you write.

SETTLING THE WEST

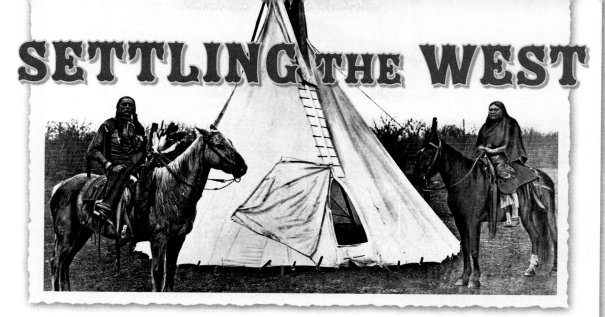

Settling in the American West took bravery and staying power. Men, women, and children traveled by boat or wagon, taking all their goods along. They never knew when they might encounter Native Americans. If the settlers did meet them, would these people be friendly or angry?

Once they chose a plot of land, the pioneers faced many difficulties. Homesteaders were pioneers who bought cheap public land and set up farms or ranches. In the grasslands, they often had to build makeshift earthen homes. They built with dirt or sod because wood was so scarce.

Over time, their numbers grew. In time, a settlement, or community in the wilderness, was established.

Battles between settlers and Native Americans continued in many places, as the Native Americans saw their land disappearing. There were losses on both sides. The U.S. government saw the land as its own. It commissioned officers and sent troops to battle the Native Americans. After many years of conflict and negotiating, Native Americans were mostly forced into the bondage of living on reservations. They no longer had the freedom to live as they once had.

Your Turn!

 Need a Review? For help using context clues to determine the meanings of unfamiliar words, see page 115.

Ready to Try It? As you read other text, use context clues to help you determine the meanings of unfamiliar words.

Objective
• Determine the meanings of unfamiliar words by using the context of the sentence.

Envision It! | Words to Know

corrode

engulfed

hoard

characteristic

exploit

extract

READING STREET ONLINE
VOCABULARY ACTIVITIES
www.ReadingStreet.com

Vocabulary Strategy for

🎯 Unfamiliar Words

Context Clues If you find a word you do not know, check the context, or the words and sentences around the unfamiliar word. Often an author provides clues that suggest the meaning of a word.

1. Reread the sentence in which the unfamiliar word appears. Look for a specific clue to the word's meaning.

2. Think about the overall meaning of the sentence in which the unfamiliar word appears.

3. If you need more help, reread other sentences near the sentence with the unfamiliar word. They may contain enough information to suggest the word's meaning.

4. Try your meaning in the original sentence. Does it make sense? If it doesn't, consult the glossary or a dictionary.

Read "All That Glitters." Use context clues to figure out the meanings of unfamiliar words.

Words to Write Reread "All That Glitters." Then look closely at a piece of jewelry and write a description of it. Use as many words from the Words to Know list as you can.

All That Glitters

Gold and silver are the metals most often used for making jewelry. Both have a characteristic shine. Because they reflect light, people have long been drawn to both metals. However, you may know that silver will corrode. This means that its atoms mix with oxygen. Eventually, a coat of tarnish appears on the surface. The process eventually eats away the outer layer of silver. Gold does not corrode.

Both metals must be mined. That is, it is necessary to extract them from the Earth. This can only be done where they are found in a concentrated form. If the metal is not found in pure chunks, it must somehow be pulled out of the ore in which it is found.

Many people are drawn to places where large pockets of ore are discovered. Gold and silver miners hope to exploit, or profit from, the rich veins of metal. For centuries, people have wanted to gather hoards of the stuff. A stockpile of gold and silver tells the world, "I am powerful and rich!" Even usually kind people can be engulfed by greed and selfishness at the thought of getting all that gold and silver!

Your Turn!

 Need a Review? For additional help with context clues, see page 115.

▶ **Ready to Try It?** As you read other text, use what you learned about context clues to help you determine the meanings of unfamiliar words.

Objective

• Determine the meanings of unfamiliar words by using the context clues of the sentence.

architecture

empire

mythology

democracy

ideal

Vocabulary Strategy for

🎯 Unfamiliar Words

Context Clues When you come across a word you do not recognize, sometimes you can use context clues—the words and sentences around an unfamiliar word—to help you figure out the meaning of the word.

1. Read the words and sentences around the unfamiliar word. The author may give you a definition of the word or suggest a relationship that can help you predict the word's meaning.

2. If you find no clues, say to yourself what you think the sentence that contains the word means.

3. Predict a meaning for the unfamiliar word.

4. Try your predicted meaning in the sentence. Does it make sense?

5. If necessary, consult the glossary or a dictionary.

Read "Lessons from the Past." Use context clues to help you determine the meanings of unfamiliar words.

Words to Write Reread "Lessons from the Past." In which past era would you most like to have lived? Write a journal entry telling about this era and why you admire it. Use words from the Words to Know list in your journal entry.

LESSONS from the PAST

Human beings have always asked themselves: How should we live? What way of life is best? We can study the past to try to answer these questions. By asking still more questions (What kind of government has been best? When have people been happiest?), we can learn from the past. We can try to comprehend what would make up the ideal, or perfect, way of life.

Ancient civilizations have sent us messages. Their literature and histories communicate how people lived and felt. Every civilization has its mythology—a body of stories that explain the workings of the world and religion. These tales, filled with struggle, show us what ancestors believed to be the meaning of life. However, they express little happiness or contentment.

The empire was a common type of government in many past civiliza-tions. The strong rule of a single person might lead to astounding art, architecture, and invention. But most subjects were not free to enjoy these boons. Over thousands of years, humans have moved away from government with a single, all-powerful ruler toward democracy. We have come to believe that each person should be free and have a voice in how his or her community is governed.

Your Turn!

 Need a Review? For more help with context clues, see page 115.

▶ **Ready to Try It?**
As you read other text, use context clues to help determine the meanings of unfamiliar words.

Antonyms

An antonym is a word that has the opposite meaning of another word. *Day* is an antonym for *night*.

whisper

blare

Antonym = Opposite

Strategy for Antonyms

1. Identify the word for which you want to find an antonym.
2. Think of other words or phrases that have the opposite meaning.
3. Use a thesaurus to help you find antonyms.
4. Use a dictionary to check antonyms' meanings so that you use the word that best communicates your ideas.

Synonyms

Synonyms are two or more words that have the same meaning or nearly the same meaning.

display

Synonym = Sam

show

Strategy for Synonyms

1. Identify the word for which you want to find a synonym.
2. Think of other words or phrases that have the same, or almost the same, meaning.
3. Use a thesaurus to help you find more synonyms, and make a list.
4. Use a dictionary to find the word that best communicates your ideas.

Envision It! | Words to Know

lunging

slung

speckled

nub

romping

rowdy

Vocabulary Strategy for

🎯 Synonyms

Thesaurus A synonym is a word that has the same or almost the same meaning as another word. You can find synonyms for a word by looking up the word in a thesaurus.

1. Identify the word and think about its meaning.

2. Look up the word in a thesaurus.

3. Examine the synonyms listed and consider what each of them means.

4. Use a dictionary to be sure of each synonym's exact meaning.

5. Choose the synonym that makes the best sense in the sentence.

Read "A Best Friend." Look for Words to Know that might have synonyms listed in a thesaurus. Look them up to see what the synonyms are.

Words to Write Reread "A Best Friend." Does a dog live with you? Or would you like to get a dog? Think about fun things you can do with a dog. Write a description of how you and a dog might play. Use words from the Words to Know list in your description.

A Best Friend

The bond between people and dogs runs deep and strong. Owners just fall in love with their dogs. These four-legged friends return the feeling many times over. The size, shape, and breed of the dog do not seem to matter. It might be a speckled, sleek Dalmatian. It might be a stubby-legged, wiry-haired Scottie with a nub of a tail. All dogs adore their people.

Romping with the kids on the lawn, the family dog shows joy with its whole body. Lunging for a tossed ball in the park, it leaps higher and farther than muscles should allow. Happiness seems to give the dog extra lift. Even a quiet old dog sitting by its master's feet seems to want nothing more.

Worn out after a shared run or walk, owner and dog lie down together for a nap. A child sleeps with a trusting arm slung over the dog's back. This picture says a lot about the connection we feel with these family members with fur. Whether the time together has been rowdy or calm, the dog is content. It seems to say with every inch of its being, nothing makes me happier than spending time with you!

Your Turn!

 Need a Review? For additional help with synonyms, see page 129.

▶ **Ready to Try It?** As you read other text, use what you learned about synonyms to help you understand it.

Objectives
• Determine the meanings of unfamiliar words by using the context of the sentence.

Envision It! | Words to Know

frantic

stunned

treaded

customary

emphasized

Vocabulary Strategy for

Synonyms

Context Clues When you find a word you do not know, look at words near it. Often the author will provide clues to help you figure out the meaning of the word. One kind of clue is a synonym, a word or phrase that means the same or almost the same thing.

1. Reread the sentence in which the unknown word appears.

2. Look for another word or words that give a clue to the word's meaning.

3. Are two things being compared? Look for nearby words that point to similarity, such as *like, also,* or *similarly.*

4. Identify the synonym and think about its meaning.

5. See if this meaning can be substituted for the unknown word. Does the sentence make sense?

Read "Water Safety at the Beach." Look for synonyms to help you figure out the meanings of words.

Words to Write Reread "Water Safety at the Beach." Write what you know about keeping safe in another dangerous situation. Use words from the Words to Know list in your writing.

Water Safety at the Beach

A day at the beach sounds relaxing and fun. Who doesn't enjoy building sand castles, napping, and splashing in the blue-green water? However, if you choose to swim in the ocean, find out about what may be waiting in the waters.

It is customary for a beach to post a sign with any important information about swimming there. On the usual list, safety rules are emphasized. The sign may also focus on when and where the water becomes deep and whether there are riptides, which are dangerous currents that flow swiftly outward from the shore.

People are often stunned to learn that a riptide can pull a good swimmer far out to sea in minutes. Many fight the current, trying to swim against it back to the beach. They become frantic as they see they are losing ground. Despite their frenzied work, they move farther out to sea. Too late, a swimmer may realize that he or she should have treaded water to save strength. The best strategy is to swim at an angle to the current. Passing beyond it, the swimmer can then safely swim back toward shore.

Your Turn!

Need a Review? For additional help with synonyms, see page 129.

Ready to Try It? As you read other text, use what you learned about synonyms to help you understand what you read.

133

Envision It! Words to Know

pawn

remote

rummage

reception

resume

rustling

simultaneous

Vocabulary Strategy for

 **Antonyms**

Context Clues When you find a word you do not know, you can often figure out its meaning by finding a clue in the words around it. The writer may include an antonym, or a word with the opposite meaning, as a clue.

1. Read the sentence in which the unfamiliar word appears.

2. Look for a word or phrase that gives a clue to its meaning.

3. Are two things being contrasted? Look for words that point to opposites, such as *unlike, however, but,* or *instead of.*

4. Determine the meaning of the antonym.

5. Give the unfamiliar word the opposite meaning of the antonym. Does this meaning make sense in the sentence?

Read "Lost and Found." Look for antonyms that may give you clues to unfamiliar words' meanings.

Words to Write Reread "Lost and Found." When have you lost something that was important to you? Write a short journal entry to explain. Use words from the Words to Know list in your journal entry.

Lost and Found

It had been an absolutely horrible day. Oscar had lost his prize-winning essay, and he had no idea where it might be. The essay topic was *Literary Elements of The Swiss Family Robinson,* and he was eager to show it to his own family.

Oscar had only discovered the loss when he'd dumped his books out of his backpack at home, rustling through papers as he looked. His sister and her friend had been of little help. They were playing chess, and his sister was very focused on where she'd next move her pawn. His little brother was busy, too, playing with his remote-controlled car.

Simultaneously, instead of separately, his sister and her friend waved an absent-minded good-bye as Oscar raced out the door. After tracing his steps to school and back, he found nothing. In a last desperate effort, he rummaged through his backpack again, looking through every folder and book. No luck.

Then, just as he was about to resume his search outdoors, Oscar stopped. He remembered that he'd returned a library book on the way home. He grabbed his phone and called the library. Because of the storm, reception wasn't very good. Still, he frantically explained—and then waited for the librarian to come back to the phone. Hooray! The essay was inside the returned book! Oscar raced out the door again. This time he knew exactly where he was going.

Your Turn!

⏸ **Need a Review?** For additional help with antonyms, see page 128.

▶ **Ready to Try It?** As you read other text, use what you learned about antonyms to help you understand it.

135

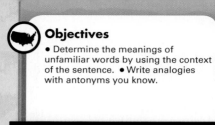

Objectives
• Determine the meanings of unfamiliar words by using the context of the sentence. • Write analogies with antonyms you know.

Words to Know

decline

former

unaccompanied

accustomed

presence

Vocabulary Strategy for

🎯 Antonyms

Context Clues Antonyms are words that mean the opposite of one another. You can use analogies, or comparisons that show relationships, to help you understand antonyms. For example, *tall* is to *short* as *few* is to *many*. Sometimes a writer uses an antonym near an unfamiliar word to help readers understand the unfamiliar word.

1. Reread the words and sentences around the unfamiliar word. Are two things being contrasted? Look for words and phrases that point to opposites such as *unlike, not, however, but,* and *on the other hand.*

2. If there is an antonym, think about a word that means the opposite and substitute it for the unfamiliar word.

3. Does this meaning make sense in the sentence?

4. If not, look up the unfamiliar word in the dictionary.

Read "An Invitation to a Wedding." Look for antonyms that help you understand the meanings of any unfamiliar words.

Words to Write Reread "An Invitation to a Wedding." Then write a description of a wedding you have attended or watched on TV. Use as many words from the Words to Know list as you can.

An Invitation to a Wedding

The invitation began "Mr. and Mrs. Harold Smith request the honor of your presence. . . ." I thought to myself, *Oh, no! Not another wedding!* And I began thinking of ways to excuse myself from this celebration.

I didn't always feel this way. I enjoyed the joyous occasion and the party that followed as much as the next person. But as I grew older, my enthusiasm for weddings went into a decline. The more friends and cousins married, the more people asked me, "Isn't it time that you get married?" If I attended a wedding unaccompanied, people shot me sympathetic glances.

(*Poor thing,* they thought. *All alone again.*) If I escorted a friend to the wedding, we were at once claimed by the hordes of matchmak-ers who seem to live for weddings. (*Have you set a date yet?*)

One day I'll meet the right person. Then I'll be ready to take my turn in front of the well-wishers. My former distaste for weddings will dissolve as I relish my own future wedding. By then, my family will have become so accustomed to my single state that it will be hard for them to get used to the idea that I'm getting married!

Your Turn!

 Need a Review? For additional help with antonyms, see page 128.

▶ **Ready to Try It?** As you read other text, use what you've learned about antonyms to help you under-stand it.

137

Objectives
• Determine the meanings of unfamiliar words by using the context of the sentence. • Use a thesaurus to locate information about words.

Envision It! | Words to Know

densest

eaves

moisture

expanse

ventured

Vocabulary Strategy for

Synonyms

Context Clues Synonyms are two or more words that mean almost the same thing. An author may use a synonym near a difficult word to help you understand the difficult word's meaning.

1. Read the words and sentences around the unfamiliar word.

2. Look for clues that indicate the unfamiliar word has a synonym. A synonym is often preceded by the word *or* or *like,* and it may be set off by commas.

3. If you find a synonym, try using it in place of the unfamiliar word. This will help you understand the meaning.

4. If this does not help you understand the word, read on or look up the word in the glossary or a dictionary.

Read "Tropical Rain Forest." Use context clues to identify synonyms for unfamiliar words or, if you can't find them on your own, consult a thesaurus and a dictionary.

Words to Write Reread "Tropical Rain Forest." Imagine an animal living in a tropical rain forest. Write a paragraph describing a typical day in its life. Use words from the Words to Know list as you write.

Tropical Rain Forest

The tropical rain forest is a green super-city. We think of cities as being crowded places, but rain forests have the densest, or most crowded, populations of living things. A city may grow to hold many millions of people, but the world's rain forests contain nearly half the world's species, or kinds, of plants as well as a huge variety of animals.

Those who have ventured into the rain forest know that its vast expanse, or area, includes towering trees and miles of long vines. Under the eaves of these giants, many kinds of ferns, mosses, flowers, and shrubs grow. Because it gets so much moisture—from as little as 80 inches to as much as 250 inches of rainfall each year—and warmth, a tropical rain forest is always lush and green.

Of course, animals of all kinds love it there—fish, frogs, birds, snakes, and monkeys, to name a few. Insects, however, are by far the most plentiful animals in the rain forest.

Your Turn!

II Need a Review? For additional help with synonyms, see page 129.

▶ Ready to Try It?
As you read other text, use what you learned about synonyms to help you understand it.

burden

rural

urban

conformed

leisure

maintenance

sufficient

Vocabulary Strategy for

Synonyms

Context Clues When you find a word you do not know, look at words near the unfamiliar word. Often the author will provide clues to help you figure out the word's meaning. One kind of clue is a synonym, a word with the same or almost the same meaning as another word.

1. Read the words and sentences near the unfamiliar word. The author may give you a synonym of the word that can help you predict the word's meaning. Authors sometimes use synonyms in their writing to help define more difficult words.

2. Look for a synonym of the unfamiliar word. Substitute the synonym in place of the word. Does this meaning make sense in the sentence?

3. If not, read on. The larger context may make the meaning clear.

4. If you still cannot find the definition of the unfamiliar word, use a dictionary.

Read "Country Versus City." Use synonyms to help you figure out the meanings of unfamiliar words.

Words to Write Reread "Country Versus City." Look at the picture in the selection and describe it. Use as many words from the Words to Know list as you can.

Country Versus City

The twentieth century was a time of great change in the United States. In this time, America began the change from a more rural country to one that had larger and larger urban populations. In the early 1900s, most Americans lived on small farms in the country. But in large cities, industry was growing. However, world wars placed a burden, or hardship, on supplies of everything. The nation began to build more factories, and production of goods was stepped up. People were needed to work in the factories, so many people who had worked in smaller rural areas moved to urban centers, where the jobs were.

Some of these migrants had troubles. For example, an influx of workers could mean there was not sufficient, or enough, housing. Families crowded into small apartments. They were not responsible for the maintenance, or upkeep, of the apartments. Even so, the building owner might not make needed repairs. Life in the city meant changes in lifestyle. For example, what people did with their leisure, or free, time changed. Cities offered more action but less space.

As the century wore on and America became richer and more productive, urban populations became more sophisticated. Their interests conformed to, or matched up with, the opportunities they had come to know—better libraries, theaters, and other social and educational resources.

Your Turn!

 Need a Review? For additional help with synonyms, see page 129.

Ready to Try It? As you read other text, use what you learned about synonyms to help you understand it.

Prefixes

A prefix is a word part added onto the front of a base word to form a new word.

cap

uncap

Strategy for Prefixes

1. Look at the unknown word and identify the prefix.
2. What does the base word mean? If you're not sure, check a dictionary.
3. Use what you know about the base word and the prefix to figure out the meaning of the unknown word.
4. Use a dictionary to check your guess.

Common Prefixes and Their Meanings

Prefix	Meaning
un-	not
re-	again, back
in-	not
dis-	not, opposite of
pre-	before

Suffixes

A suffix is a word part added to the end of a base word to form a new word.

coat

coatless

Common Suffixes and Their Meanings

Suffix	Meaning
-ly	characteristic of
-ation	act, process
-able	can be done
-ment	action or process
-less	without

Strategy for Suffixes

1. Look at the unknown word and identify the suffix.
2. What does the base word mean? If you're not sure, check a dictionary.
3. Use what you know about the base word and the suffix to figure out the meaning of the unknown word.
4. Use a dictionary to check your guess.

Objectives
● Understand the purpose of suffixes in changing the meanings of words.

Envision It! | Words to Know

morsel

ruff

stooped

fixed

furious

nudge

quietly

vigil

Vocabulary Strategy for

🎯 Suffixes *-ly, -ous*

Word Structure When you are reading and come across a word you don't know, check to see if the word has a suffix at its end. Suffixes add meaning. For example, *-ly* means "a characteristic of," as in *honestly*, and *-ous* means "having much" or "full of," as in *adventurous*. The meaning of the suffix combines with the meaning of the base word.

Choose one of the Words to Know and follow these steps.

1. Cover the suffix and identify the base form of the word.

2. If you know this word, think about its meaning.

3. Look at the suffix and decide what extra meaning it adds.

4. Combine the meanings from steps 2 and 3.

5. Use this meaning in the sentence. Does it make sense?

Read "Jack to the Rescue." Look for words that end with the suffixes *-ly* and *-ous*. Analyze the base words and the suffixes to figure out meaning.

Words to Write Reread "Jack to the Rescue." Think about a time when you observed a scene in a public place. Imagine you are waiting in that place and describe what you see. Use as many words from the Words to Know list as you can.

Jack to the Rescue

I sat in the park watching the ducks feed. The ducks made a furious noise as people fed morsels to them. Just then, a little boy ran down the path. He looked about three. A duck waddled into the pond. The little boy boldly started to follow him.

As I jumped up to stop him, a Husky raced to the boy. The dog stepped between the boy and the pond. "Jack!" cried the boy, grabbing Jack's ruff.

Jack used his nose to nudge the boy away from the pond. He kept nudging until the boy toddled to a sandbox filled with children that was just past the pond.

The boy played happily in the sandbox. Jack sat quietly, never taking his eyes off the child.

Suddenly I heard a woman in a quavering voice call, "Has anyone seen my son? He disappeared when I went over to pick up his toys." She was stooped over with fear.

Jack barked, but he did not take his eyes off the boy. The woman rushed over to the sandbox and ran to the boy. Her reaction was to hug him and then lead him away.

Once Jack's vigil was over, he came over to me. He fixed his eyes on my sandwich. I gave him the whole thing. I realized that he had earned it. Then he ran off to be with his family.

Your Turn!

❚❚ **Need a Review?** For additional help with suffixes, see page 143.

▶ **Ready to Try It?** As you read other text, use what you learned about suffixes to help you understand it.

Objectives
• Identify the meanings of common suffixes and how they change words' meanings. • Use knowledge of word structure to help determine a word's meaning.

Envision It! Words to Know

excavated

pottery

terra cotta

approximately

divine

mechanical

restore

superstitious

watchful

Vocabulary Strategy for

Suffixes -al, -ful, and -ly

Word Structure When you are reading and come across a word you don't know, check to see if the word has a suffix, or word part added to the end of the word. Suffixes add meaning. For example, -al means "of" or "like"; -ful means "full of" or "showing"; and -ly means "in a way" or "of or from." The suffixes -al and -ful change a noun into an adjective; -ly changes an adjective into an adverb.

Choose one of the Words to Know and follow these steps.

1. Cover the suffix and see if you recognize the base word.

2. If you know this word, think about its meaning.

3. Look at the suffix. Think about its meaning and how it changes the meaning of the base word.

4. Decide what meaning makes sense for the word.

Read "Discovering Artifacts." Use suffixes and word structure to help you figure out the meanings of any unfamiliar words you find.

Words to Write Reread "Discovering Artifacts." Write a description of what you imagine you might see during a trip to a natural history museum. Use as many words from the Words to Know list as you can.

Discovering Artifacts

Last week we went to visit a museum that has approximately two thousand artifacts from ancient China. Most of the things we saw were made by humans thousands of years ago. How cool is that!

We started the day by watching a video about how archaeologists carefully uncover pottery. They use mechanical equipment and dig into the ground. Somehow they manage not to break the excavated objects. Some pottery in the video reminded me of the terra cotta flowerpots at my grandmother's house. The film ended with a look at how specialists work to restore any damaged pieces.

After the film, we walked around to see several displays. I kept a watchful eye for something about the first emperor of China. I had read that he considered himself to be divine and the ruler of everyone. The museum did not have anything from the emperor's mausoleum, but I did read an interesting description about the superstitious fears many people used to have about the emperor's terra cotta army.

Your Turn!

 Need a Review?
For additional help with suffixes, see page 143.

▶ **Ready to Try It?**
As you read other text, use what you learned about suffixes to help you understand it.

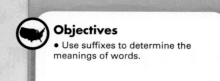
application

enraged

recital

dramatic	formal
momentous	opera
prejudice	
privileged	

Vocabulary Strategy for

Suffixes *-ic, -ous, -ation*

Word Structure A suffix is a word part added to the end of a base word that changes its meaning, the way it is used in a sentence, and sometimes how it is spelled. The suffix *-ic* adds the meaning "pertaining to or associated with," as in *romantic*. The suffix *-ous* adds the meaning "full of," as in *joyous*. The suffix *-ation* makes a noun out of a verb, usually adding the meaning "the state of being," as in *starvation*. Knowing the meaning of a suffix may help you figure out the meaning of a word.

1. Look at the word. See if you recognize a base word in it.

2. Check to see if the suffix *-ic, -ous,* or *-ation* has been added to the base word.

3. Ask yourself how the added suffix changes the meaning of the base word.

4. See if your meaning makes sense in the sentence.

As you read "From a Different Planet?" use what you know about the suffixes *-ic, -ous,* and *-ation* to figure out the meanings of words.

Words to Write Reread "From a Different Planet?" Select one of the examples given of dramatic moments and write about it. Use as many words from the Words to Know list as you can.

From a Different Planet?

The world of opera is much like another planet to some people. Not only do they have a difficult time trying to understand it, but they also try to avoid it. Admittedly, this mixture of drama and music is much too formal for the taste of many Americans. Opera is quite different from other forms of recital and concert that some people are more familiar with. However, the roots of prejudice against this art form are fed by other oddities.

To begin with, opera is usually sung in a language other than English. That means we are privileged to get to see opera because it opens our eyes to another culture and language. Attending an opera is meant to be enjoyable, not like filling out a job application!

Another fault we find with opera is actually one of its great strengths. It forces us to look at momentous occasions in someone's life. It takes a dramatic moment and multiplies its feelings times ten. Love brings the greatest joy. Loss brings awful sadness and even death. Jealousy drives an enraged lover to murder. The pageant of life is acted out before us with great feeling and color. If we can learn to live in this intense world for a few hours, we come away richer in spirit.

Your Turn!

 Need a Review?
For additional help using suffixes, see page 143.

 Ready to Try It?
As you read other text, use what you learned about suffixes to help you understand it.

confidently

dismounted

flourish

distressed

fulfill

permission

repay

vigorously

Vocabulary Strategy for

🔄 Prefixes *re-* and *dis-*

Word Structure When you come across a word you do not know, see if the word begins with a prefix that might help you to figure out the meaning of the word. For example, the prefix *re-* usually adds the meaning "again" to a word, as in *reschedule*, or "back," as in *rewind*. Usually, the prefix *dis-* adds the meaning "to remove" or "the opposite of," as in *disrespect*. Follow these steps when you come across a word that has a prefix.

1. Cover the prefix.

2. Look at the base word. See if you know what it means.

3. Uncover the prefix. Think about its meaning.

4. Combine the meaning of the prefix with the meaning of the base word.

5. Check the context. Does this meaning make sense in this sentence?

Read "Kindness for Kindness." Use prefixes to help you figure out the meanings of the words.

Words to Write Reread "Kindness for Kindness." What could you do to help someone you love? Write about your plan. Use as many words from the Words to Know list as you can.

Kindness for Kindness

As she rode along the lane, Terry tried to think of a way to repay Miss Posy. The elderly woman had been the one to fulfill Terry's dream of owning her own horse. Miss Posy had offered Terry a job cleaning stalls and grooming horses on her dude ranch. After a year, Terry had enough money to buy Biscuit from Miss Posy. He was old but gentle and easy to ride, and Terry loved the horse to an unreasonable degree.

Arriving at the ranch after a ride, Terry dismounted and put Biscuit in a pasture to graze. Then she got to work. Terry moved confidently among the horses in the barn. As she vigorously forked clean straw into stalls, she thought of something she could do for her employer.

Last winter, Miss Posy had suffered a stroke and now spent much of her time sitting on the porch. This distressed Terry, who knew how much Miss Posy loved walking outdoors. Smiling, Terry marched to the porch and got permission for her project. Soon a beautiful big garden of flowers began to flourish next to Miss Posy's porch.

Your Turn!

 Need a Review? For additional help using prefixes, see page 142.

▶ **Ready to Try It?** As you read other text, use what you learned about prefixes to help you understand it.

Objectives
• Determine the meanings of English words formed with prefixes from Latin and other languages. • Use knowledge of word structure to help determine a word's meaning.

Envision It! | Words to Know

percentage

reproduce

transmitted

converts

devise

efficiency

generated

proclaimed

Vocabulary Strategy for

🎯 Prefixes *re-, pro-,* and *trans-*

Word Structure A prefix is a word part that is added to the beginning of a base, or root, word. The prefix changes the base word's meaning. When you come across an unfamiliar word with a prefix, knowing the meaning of the prefix can help you to figure out the word. The prefix *re-* means "again"; *pro-* means "forth" or "forward"; and *trans-* means "across," "beyond," or "through."

1. Look at an unfamiliar word to see if it has a base word you know.

2. Check to see if the prefix *re-, pro-,* or *trans-* has been added to the base word.

3. Think about what meaning the prefix adds to the meaning of the base word.

4. Try the meaning and the base word together.

5. See if the meaning you come up with makes sense in the sentence. If it doesn't, look up the word in a glossary or a dictionary.

Read "Hats Off to Inventors." Look for words that have prefixes. Use the prefixes to help you figure out the meanings of the words.

Words to Write Reread "Hats Off to Inventors." Choose an invention you think is important. Write about how it has changed people's lives. Use as many words from the Words to Know list as you can.

Hats Off to Inventors

We owe the comfort and convenience of our lives to inventors. These creative geniuses devise better ways to do or make something. Sometimes this means coming up with a whole new invention, such as the telephone. Thanks to this machine, sound is transmitted over great distances. At other times, inventors have just improved the efficiency of a machine that already exists. The radial tire, for example, meant that cars would get better gas mileage. Even simple inventions can make a big difference. For example, the sticky-note converts paper into a message that can be placed right where you want it. The inventor is a practical dreamer. He or she wants to make a product that is easy to reproduce and useful so that the public will buy it.

Inventors have been around for thousands of years, but in the last 150 years they have generated by far the greatest percentage of new gadgets ever invented. In many ways, their work has made life better for us all. Don't you think a special Inventors Day should be proclaimed?

Your Turn!

 Need a Review? For additional help with prefixes, see page 142.

▶ **Ready to Try It?** As you read other text, use what you learned about prefixes to help you understand it.

Objectives
• Determine the meanings of English words that have Latin affixes.

Envision It! Words to Know

lance

misfortune

squire

quests

renewed

renowned

resound

READING STREET ONLINE
VOCABULARY ACTIVITIES
www.ReadingStreet.com

Vocabulary Strategy for

Prefixes *re-* and *mis-*

Word Structure When you come across a word you do not know, one way to figure out its meaning is to understand the meanings of its parts. An affix— a prefix or suffix—is a syllable added to a base word that changes the base word's meaning. The prefix *re-* means "again" or "back," as in *retell* and *recall*. The prefix *mis-* means "bad" or "wrong," as in *misbehave* or *misspell*.

Choose one of the Words to Know and follow these steps.

1. Identify the prefix.

2. Cover the prefix and look at the base word. Think about its meaning.

3. Uncover the prefix and identify its meaning.

4. Add the prefix's meaning to the meaning of the base word.

5. Check the context. Does this meaning make sense in this sentence?

Read "Knights of Old." Look for words that have prefixes. Use the prefixes to help you figure out the meanings of the words.

Words to Write Reread "Knights of Old." Imagine that you are watching two knights battle. Describe the scene. Use as many words from the Words to Know list as you can.

KNIGHTS OF OLD

Medieval knights were actually soldiers, not just the brave heroes of adventure stories. Stories tell us that knights went on quests. A knight might fight an evil beast or save a fair lady whom misfortune had placed in danger. In spite of great hardship, he always renewed his devotion and carried on. One of the most renowned of these legendary knights was Lancelot.

Real knights did go through a ceremony in which they promised to use their weapons for noble causes and high ideals. A boy who was to become a knight first served as a squire. At fifteen or sixteen he became the personal servant of a knight. He trained hard and rode with his master into battle. Knights wore heavy armor and used a lance as well as a sword to fight.

Knights sometimes fought in tournaments, which at first were much like battles. The air would resound with the clanging of swords. Over time, the contests changed. Pairs of knights would square off and try to unseat each other using blunt lances. Today, fights similar to these are sometimes re-created for educational and entertainment purposes.

Your Turn!

⏸ Need a Review? For additional help with prefixes, see page 142.

▶ Ready to Try It? As you read other text, use what you learned about prefixes to help you understand it.

Dictionary

A dictionary is a reference book that lists words alphabetically. It can be used to look up pronunciation, parts of speech, definitions, and spelling of words.

punc•tu•al ❶ (pungk′ chü əl), ❷ *ADJECTIVE.* ❸ prompt; exactly on time: ❹ *He is always punctual.* ❺ ✸ *ADVERB* **punc′tu•al•ly.**

❶ Pronunciation

❷ Part of speech

❸ Definitions

❹ Example sentence

❺ Other form of the word and its part of speech

Strategy for Dictionary

1. Identify the unknown word.
2. Look up the word in a dictionary. Entries are listed alphabetically.
3. Find the part of the entry that has the information you are looking for.
4. Use the diagram above as a guide to help you locate the information you want.

Thesaurus

A thesaurus is a book of synonyms. A thesaurus may also list antonyms for many words.

cute
adjective
attractive, appealing, amusing, charming, adorable, enchanting.
ANTONYMS: plain, ugly

Strategy for Thesaurus

1. Look up the word in a thesaurus. Entries are listed alphabetically.
2. Locate the synonyms and any antonyms for your word.
3. Use a dictionary to help you choose the word with the exact meaning you want.

Objectives
• Use a dictionary or glossary to locate information about words.
• Determine the meanings of unfamiliar words by using the context of the sentence.

Envision It! | Words to Know

alcoves

obsidian

pueblo

decades

prehistoric

trowels

Vocabulary Strategy for

Unknown Words

Dictionary/Glossary When you are reading and come across a word you do not know, first try to use context clues to figure out its meaning. If that doesn't work, look up the word in a dictionary or glossary.

Choose one of the Words to Know and follow these steps.

1. Look in a dictionary.

2. Find the entry for the word. The entries in a dictionary are in alphabetical order.

3. Use the pronunciation key to pronounce the word.

4. Read all of the meanings given for the word.

5. Choose the meaning that makes sense in your sentence.

Read "A Door into the Past." Use context clues before you consult a dictionary to determine the meanings of unknown words.

Words to Write Reread "A Door into the Past." Think of a building or location that is part of your community's history. Do some research to find out the facts about it. Then write about this place, using as many words from the Words to Know list as you can.

A Door into the Past

"Today we are going to my secret fishing spot," said Grandpa.

"I don't like to fish," I complained.

Grandpa winked. "If you can sacrifice one day with your friends, you'll learn that the fishing spot is not my only secret."

After a hike we headed down a long, steep slope. "My fishing spot is at the bottom," said Grandpa.

Halfway down, he picked up an arrowhead made of obsidian. He pointed to an alcove cut into a cliff face. I saw a grinding stone on the ground with a few corncobs next to it.

"How did you know about this place?" I asked.

"It's on the way to my fishing spot. I've been coming here for decades," he said. "I think I'm the only one who knows it's here. I knew you were interested in archaeology, so it was time to show you. What prehistoric people lived here, do you think?"

"The early Pueblo," I said. "They lived in alcoves before they began building pueblos near a kiva."

"That was my guess too," said Grandpa. "All these years, I have wanted to share this with just the right person."

Then he opened his fishing pack. Inside were two trowels wrapped in cloth. "Someday we will do more exploring here. But now, let's fish!"

Your Turn!

⏸ **Need a Review?** For additional help with using a dictionary, see page 156.

▶ **Ready to Try It?** As you read other text, use a dictionary or glossary to find the meanings of unknown words.

Objective
• Use a dictionary or glossary to determine the meanings of and locate information about unknown words.

Envision It! | **Words to Know**

captive

companionship

sanctuaries

existence

ordeal

primitive

stimulating

READING STREET ONLINE
VOCABULARY ACTIVITIES
www.ReadingStreet.com

Vocabulary Strategy for

Unknown Words

Dictionary/Glossary When you come across a word you do not know, first see if you can use context clues to figure out the meaning. If that doesn't work, use a dictionary or glossary for help.

Choose one of the Words to Know and follow these steps.

1. Look in a dictionary.

2. Find the entry for the word. The entries in dictionaries are listed in alphabetical order.

3. Use the pronunciation key to pronounce the word.

4. Read all the meanings given for the word.

5. Choose the meaning that makes sense.

Read "Zoos Then and Now" on page 161. Look for context clues to help you figure out the meanings of unknown words before you turn to a dictionary.

Words to Write Reread "Zoos Then and Now." Look at the photograph of the two orangutans on page 161. Write a paragraph about what you think their life might be like inside a modern zoo. Use as many words from the Words to Know list as you can.

Zoos Then and Now

The first zoos existed to entertain people, who came to see strange, wild animals from around the world. Hardly anyone thought about the health and happiness of these captive animals. For the most part, they were kept in small cages. Little was known about them, so no one knew what they needed for food or homes. Zoo life was nothing like their existence in the wild. Being shut in a tiny space and looking at metal and concrete all day was surely an ordeal.

Today, zoos are very different from those early, primitive places. Zoos today try hard to make life interesting and "normal" for their animals. The best zoos provide environments like those the animals would have in the wild. They offer many stimulating objects to keep the animals from getting bored. Animals are grouped in ways that make sure they have companionship. One aim is to set up family groups so babies can be born, helping endangered species increase their numbers. Zoos have become important to the survival of many animals. They are both sanctuaries and places of learning. They offer a safe place for animals to live and opportunities for people to understand the Earth's creatures.

Your Turn!

⏸ **Need a Review?** For additional help with using a dictionary, see page 156.

▶ **Ready to Try It?** As you read other text, use a dictionary or glossary to find the meanings of unknown words.

Objectives
• Use a dictionary or a glossary to determine the meanings of and to locate information about unknown words.

Unknown Words

Dictionary/Glossary When you come across a word you don't know and can't use context clues to figure out the word's meaning, use a dictionary or glossary for help.

Choose one of the Words to Know and follow these steps.

1. Open a dictionary.

2. Find the entry for the word. Entries in both places are in alphabetical order.

3. Read all the meanings given for the word.

4. Choose the meaning that makes the best sense.

Read "An Environmentally Friendly Vacation." Use a dictionary to help you determine the meanings of this week's Words to Know.

Words to Write Reread "An Environmentally Friendly Vacation." Find any other unknown words in the selection. Using a dictionary, find and write definitions for those unknown words.

Envision It! | Words to Know

emissions

forecaster

turbines

consequences
ferocious
incubator
sustainable

An Environmentally Friendly Vacation

My mother had a great idea for our vacation this year—an ecotourism trip to Costa Rica! Mom explained that ecotourism is environmentally friendly traveling. Costa Rica is a country in Central America that has a lot of ecotourism. Mom found a hotel there that is sustainable, which means it is able to serve its guests without harmful consequences to the environment. The more Mom told me about the hotel, the more excited I became. It is on a hill on the edge of the jungle. The hotel gets all its electricity from solar panels and wind turbines that look like big metal windmills made with huge airplane propellers. We will get around on bicycles instead of in cars, so we won't cause any greenhouse-gas emissions.

At the hotel, we will learn about the local culture and the plants and animals in the jungle. Mom read that sometimes the hotel workers find abandoned toucan eggs, and they keep them warm and hatch them in incubators! I'd love to know what a toucan chick looks like. It's a good thing I'm taking my camera.

I am so excited about our trip that I get on the Internet every day to look up the weather in Costa Rica. A big, ferocious storm has passed, and the forecasters are saying that next week will be sunny and warm. Mom planned our vacation carefully, and I can't help thinking that she even planned the weather!

Your Turn!

Need a Review? For additional help using a dictionary, see page 156.

Ready to Try It? As you read other text, use what you learned about using a dictionary or glossary to help you understand it.

Multiple-Meaning Words

Multiple-meaning words are words that have different meanings depending on how they are used. Homographs, homonyms, and homophones are all multiple-meaning words.

Homographs

Homographs are words that are spelled the same but have different meanings and are sometimes pronounced differently.

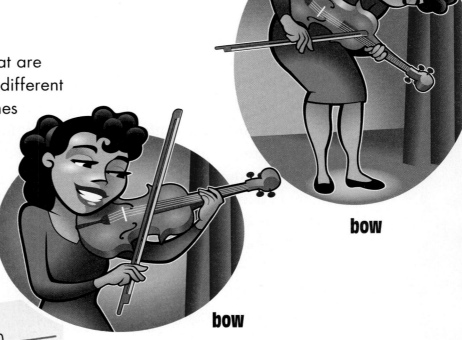

bow

bow

Some Common Homographs

bass
close
contract
lead
live
present

Strategy for Homographs

1. Read the words and phrases near the homograph.
2. Think about the homograph's different meanings and decide which one makes the most sense in the sentence.
3. Reread the sentence with your guess to see if it makes sense.
4. Check your guess in a dictionary.

Homonyms

Homonyms are words that are pronounced the same and have the same spelling, but their meanings are different.

row

row

Strategy for Homonyms

1. Read the words and phrases near the homonym.
2. Think about the homonym's different meanings and decide which one makes the most sense.
3. Reread the sentence with your guess to see if it makes sense.
4. Use a dictionary to check your guess.

Some Common
Homonyms

pen
duck
mail
ear
bank
bark

165

Homophones

Homophones are words that are pronounced the same way but have different spellings and meanings.

flour

flower

Some Common Homophones

ate	eight
bored	board
brake	break
knight	night
weight	wait

Strategy for Homophones

1. Think about the different spellings and meanings of the homophone.
2. Check a dictionary for the definitions of the words.
3. Use the word that best fits your purpose.

This chart can help you remember the differences between homographs, homonyms, and homophones.

Understanding Homographs, Homonyms, and Homophones

	Pronunciation	Spelling	Meaning
Homographs	may be the same or different	same	different
Homonyms	same	same	different
Homophones	same	different	different

Homograph

dove

dove

Homonym

mail

mail

hangar

Homophone

hanger

Objective

● Determine the meanings of multiple-meaning words by using the context of the sentence.

Envision It! | Words to Know

hatch

submersible

tentacles

ego

intrepid

propulsion

silt

READING STREET ONLINE
VOCABULARY ACTIVITIES
www.ReadingStreet.com

Vocabulary Strategy for

Multiple-Meaning Words

Context Clues Some words have more than one meaning. You can use the words and sentences around a multiple-meaning word to figure out which meaning the author is using.

1. Read the words and sentences around the multiple-meaning word.

2. Think about the possible meanings of the word. For example, *refrain* can mean "to keep oneself back" or "a phrase repeated over and over."

3. Decide which meaning makes sense in the sentence. For example, "Everyone said the same *refrain*." Reread the sentence and think of the the meaning you chose.

4. Does this meaning make sense? If not, try another meaning.

Read "Exploration!" on page 169. Use context clues to determine the meanings of any multiple-meaning words you find.

Words to Write Reread "Exploration!" What do you think it would be like to take a tour of an underwater cavern? Write a description of what you imagine, using as many words from the Words to Know list as you can.

168

Exploration!

I couldn't wait to join my aunt, a famous underwater explorer, for a trip to explore underwater caverns. I knew we would slide into the small submersible and dip down into the caverns and see extraordinary sights!

We'd have to start our trip in a large submarine, but then we could use the submersible's strong propulsion to jet away from the large craft. I knew we'd have to plug in some of the equipment pieces, like flashlights and recorders, to charge them before leaving the submarine. The power sources in the submersible were limited, and it would be important to have all of the equipment ready at a moment's notice.

I'd developed a pretty healthy ego and had bragged to all of my classmates about the trip. I knew they all wished they could go along with me, but I was the only one who would be the intrepid young sailor on this trip. I was absolutely fearless, and I was ready to open the hatch and race into the submarine to head out on the voyage.

I knew that once we landed, we would stir up fine grains of silt, but we had all the equipment to be prepared. We were even ready to deal with any tentacles that an octopus or squid might try to wrap around our submersible. What a story I would have to share when I got back to school!

Your Turn!

 Need a Review? For additional help with multiple-meaning words, see pages 164–167.

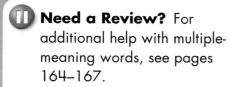 **Ready to Try It?** As you read other text, use what you learned about multiple-meaning words to help you understand it.

Objective
● Determine the meanings of multiple-meaning words by using the context of the sentence.

 Envision It! | **Words to Know**

authority

lush

wilt

access

obstacle

toll

torment

Vocabulary Strategy for

🎯 Homonyms

Context Clues When you come across a word you think you know but that doesn't make sense in the sentence, you may have come across a homonym. Homonyms are two or more words that are spelled the same and pronounced the same but have different meanings. For example, *lean* could mean either "thin" or "to rest against something for support." Always try to use the context—the words and sentences around the puzzling word—for clues to figure out the correct meaning of a homonym.

Follow these steps to use context to determine the meaning of homonyms.

1. Reread the sentence in which the homonym appears.

2. Look for context clues to the homonym's meaning.

3. If you need more help, read the sentences around the sentence with the homonym. Look for clues or for additional information that suggests the homonym's meaning.

4. Try the new meaning in the sentence. Does it make sense? If not, check a dictionary.

Read "Migrant Work Is No Picnic." Use context clues to figure out the meaning of any homonyms you find.

Words to Write Reread "Migrant Work Is No Picnic." Imagine that you are working as a migrant worker. Write a journal entry to tell what you feel and see. Use as many words from the Words to Know list as you can.

Migrant Work Is No Picnic

We tend to think of farm work as being healthful. You get fresh air and sunshine and use your muscles. You can lean against your hoe and look at the lush green crops growing in straight rows. It sounds like a satisfactory life, doesn't it?

On the contrary, for migrant workers field work means long hours, poor pay, and torment for the body and mind. With bare hands and bent backs, these workers labor from dawn to dusk in the hot sun. Even a plant will wilt under the sun's punishing rays without enough water. Sometimes the workers are not provided with water. They may not even have access to bathrooms. And, as for fresh air, workers instead often breathe the fumes of powerful insecticides.

All this hard labor takes a toll on workers' health. Yet they often fail to get proper health care. When your pay is scarcely enough to buy food for your family, a doctor's bills become an obstacle that can't be overcome. Getting people the authority to fight for the rights of migrant workers has been an important issue for decades.

Your Turn!

⏸ **Need a Review?** For additional help with homonyms, see page 165.

▶ **Ready to Try It?** As you read other text, use what you learned about homonyms to help you understand it.

Objective
● Determine the meanings of multiple-meaning words by using the context of the sentence.

Envision It! | Words to Know

relish

revolting

unison

disgraced

progress

promoted

retreat

Vocabulary Strategy for

⟳ Multiple-Meaning Words

Context Clues Some words have more than one meaning. You can use words and sentences near a multiple-meaning word to figure out which meaning the author is using.

1. Read the sentences near the word in question.

2. Think about the different meanings the word may have. For example, *drum* can be a musical instrument, a metal container, or the act of tapping one's fingers.

3. Decide which meaning makes sense in this sentence: He began to *drum* his fingers on the desk.

4. Reread the sentence, replacing the word with the meaning you chose.

5. If this meaning seems right, read on. If not, try another meaning.

Read "A Party for Mom." Use context clues and your knowledge to decide which meaning a multiple-meaning word has in the article. For example, does *relish* mean "a liking for something" or "a food eaten with other foods to add flavor"?

Words to Write Reread "A Party for Mom." Describe a family party or special event that you have enjoyed. Use words from the Words to Know list.

A Party for Mom

When Mom was promoted at work, our family had a party to celebrate. We were all proud of her progress in the company. She had been employed at Merritt Controls for only three years, and she had been made a manager.

I hoped Dad wasn't planning to serve any revolting foods, such as avocado or broccoli, at the party. Of all the foods I dislike, those are my least favorite. To my relief, my parents put me in charge of the chips, dip, and relish trays. My orders were to be sure that there were plenty of eye-popping green, red, and orange colors on those trays. The pickles were green. I added green food coloring to pep them up! Maraschino cherries were red, and cheese curls added an orange-yellow color. When I saw my parents' shock, I knew I had disgraced myself.

"That's not what we meant!" they sputtered in unison. They had wanted peppers, cherry tomatoes, and carrots. Then the doorbell rang. It was too late to change the trays. I beat a retreat to my room then and there. Later, I found out that because the trays were so interesting and different, they turned out to be a big hit with all the guests.

Your Turn!

⏸ **Need a Review?** For additional help with multiple-meaning words, see pages 164–167.

▶ **Ready to Try It?** As you read other text, use what you learned about multiple-meaning words to help you understand it.

173

Envision It! | Words to Know

campaigns

comrades

invaders

benefits

enrich

foreigners

READING STREET ONLINE
VOCABULARY ACTIVITIES
www.ReadingStreet.com

Vocabulary Strategy for

Multiple-Meaning Words

Dictionary/Glossary Some words have more than one meaning. If the words and sentences around a multiple-meaning word do not give clues about which meaning the author is using, refer to a dictionary or glossary.

When you come across a word that has more than one meaning, follow these steps.

1. Think about the different meanings the word can have.

2. Find the word in a dictionary. Read the definitions. Think about the way the word is used in the text.

3. Decide which meaning makes sense in the sentence.

4. Reread the sentence, replacing the word with the meaning you think fits best.

5. If this meaning seems right, read on. If not, try another meaning.

Read "The End of the Aztecs." Use a dictionary to decide which meaning fits each of the multiple-meaning words you find in the article.

Words to Write Reread "The End of the Aztecs." Write a summary of a battle or war that you have studied or read about. Use words from the Words to Know list.

The End of the Aztecs

During the 1500s, through exploration, Europe learned of the Americas. Europeans called this place across the ocean to the west the "New World." European people had long dreamed of finding a better route to the East, with its wealth of spices, silk, jewels, and gold. A good, quick route to the East would give the discoverer many trade benefits. Instead, adventurers sailed west and found the lands and native peoples of the Americas.

Natives such as the Aztecs of Mexico had a rich kingdom with much gold. These people had vast knowledge, including ways that would help to enrich the soil to provide good crops. They had built a huge city on a lake.

The Aztec civilization was both advanced and ingenious.

The Spanish, who sought riches, organized armies and ships and set sail. What must the proud Aztec people have thought of these pale-skinned foreigners? It is likely that the Aztec leader believed the Spanish leader was a god. The Aztecs offered valuable gifts and welcomed the Spanish. But the Spanish did not want to be comrades to the Aztecs. They came as invaders, not friends. Their campaigns against the Aztecs were bloody but successful. In just two years, the Aztecs were conquered and enslaved.

Your Turn!

Need a Review? For additional help with multiple-meaning words, see pages 164–167.

Ready to Try It? As you read other text, use what you learned about multiple-meaning words to help you understand it.

Base Words/Root Words

A base word, also called a root word, is a word that can't be broken into smaller words.

lock

unlock

Lock is the base word.

Strategy for Base Words

1. Look for a base word in the unknown word.
2. Determine the meaning of the base word.
3. Guess the meaning of the unknown word. Does it make sense in the sentence?
4. Check your guess in a dictionary.

176

Word Origins: Roots

Many English words contain Greek and Latin roots.

microscope

dentist

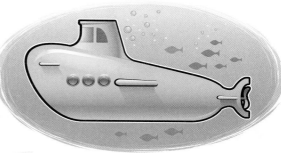

submarine

Latin Roots

dent	tooth
dict	to say; to speak
scrib	to write
sub	under; below
tract	to pull
vis	to see

Greek Roots

auto	self
bio	life
micro	very small
ology	the study of
phon	sound; voice
scope	see
tele	far

Strategy for Roots

1. Using what you know about roots, guess the meaning of the unknown word.
2. Does your guess make sense in the sentence?
3. Use a dictionary to check your guess.

Envision It! | Words to Know

fixtures

flimsy

incident

apparently

subscribe

survive

Vocabulary Strategy for
⟳ Greek and Latin Roots

Word Structure When you come across a word you don't know, look for word parts you have seen in words that you do know. Many words are built from Greek or Latin roots. For example, *scribe* is the root of the Latin word *scribere*, meaning "to write." A scribe is a person who writes. You can often figure out a word's meaning by examining its Greek or Latin root.

1. Check a word for any recognizable Greek or Latin word parts.

2. Use a dictionary to look up Greek or Latin roots you do not know.

3. Use the meaning of the root, as well as other word parts, to help you figure out the meaning of the word.

4. Reread the sentence. Does this meaning for the word make sense?

Read "Saving the Past." Look for Greek and Latin roots to help you figure out the meanings of words. You may also use a dictionary to help you figure out the meanings of the Words to Know.

Words to Write Reread "Saving the Past." What building or location in your community is a part of history? Write about this place and tell why it should never be destroyed. Use as many words from the Words to Know list as you can.

Saving the Past

Have you ever known people who are trying to save an old building from being torn down? You may have said, "So what? What's the big deal?" As far as you can see, it apparently is worthless. The roof is caving in, and the paint has faded and peeled. It looks tired and ugly and flimsy. Why not tear it down, you ask? Something cool like a mini-mall or a bicycle store could go there.

The building may be a historic landmark. You probably have several in your area. These are buildings that are rich in history. They have importance to the people of the community. Perhaps some historic incident took place there, like the birth of a President or the creation of an important invention. Maybe the building shows the details and style of a time we want to remember. Its roof, trim, and antique fixtures capture the charm of an era that is past.

Most people subscribe to the idea that we should save these buildings. They need to be preserved and treasured. While they survive, we can take pride in remembering part of who we were and are.

Your Turn!

Need a Review? For additional help with Greek and Latin roots, see page 177.

Ready to Try It? As you read other text, use what you learned about Greek and Latin roots to help you understand it.

179

Objectives

● Identify base words and their endings (including -*s* and -*ed*) and use both to figure out the meanings of unfamiliar words.

Envision It! | **Words to Know**

erosion

evaporates

tropics

basin	exported
charities	industrial
equator	recycled

Vocabulary Strategy for

🎯 Word Endings *-ed, -s*

Word Structure The endings *-ed* and *-s* may be added to verbs. The ending *-s* may also be added to nouns. It is often possible to use word endings to help you figure out the meanings of words.

1. Cover the ending and read the base word. Keep in mind that the spelling of a word sometimes changes when endings are added.

2. Reread the sentence and determine what part of speech the word is. (The ending *-s* may signal a plural noun or a present-tense, singular verb.)

3. Do you know the meaning of the verb or noun? If not, look for clues in the sentence.

4. Decide what meaning you think the word has and check to see if it makes sense in the sentence.

As you read "The Amazing Amazon," look for words that end in *-ed* or *-s*. Use the endings and the way the words are used to help you figure out their meanings.

Words to Write Reread "The Amazing Amazon." Choose one of the photos and write a description of what you see. Use words from the Words to Know list.

The Amazing Amazon

The basin of the Amazon River in South America is the area covered by the Amazon River and the rivers that flow into it. It is an area of Brazil that holds amazing wealth. Its riches lie in its vast forests. This area is part of the tropics, the land near the equator. The forests of the Amazon Basin are thought to hold millions of species of plants and animals. Many organisms can live there because of the warmth and heavy rainfall.

It rains every day in the tropical forest. Then the hot sun evaporates water from the soil and trees and other plants. This water vapor goes into the air, becomes clouds, and falls again as rain. Water is thus recycled and kept in the region. It is believed that many valuable medicines and other products can be made from the plants and animals that live there.

However, people who live in the region want to live well. They want Brazil to become an industrial nation. Many thousands of square miles of forest are being cut down every year to make way for industry. Some wood is exported, but much is burned. The tropical soil is thin, and soon erosion carries it away. Then the bare land is poor. The people often need the help of charities to help them find ways to exist without destroying their forests.

Your Turn!

Need a Review?
For additional help with base words, see page 176.

Ready to Try It?
As you read other text, use what you learned about base words and word endings to help you understand it.

astronomers

collide

galaxy

collapse

compact

particles

READING STREET ONLINE
VOCABULARY ACTIVITIES
www.ReadingStreet.com

Vocabulary Strategy for

Greek and Latin Roots

Word Structure When you find a word you do not recognize, see if you can find a familiar root in it. Greek and Latin roots, or basic original parts of words, are used in many English words. For example, the Latin root *sol* means "sun." The Greek root *astr-* means "star." The root *astr-* is used to build the words *astronaut, astrology,* and *astronomer.*

Choose one of the Words to Know and follow these steps:

1. If the word has a prefix or suffix, cover it.

2. Do you recognize the root? Does the root make a base word you know?

3. If so, see if the meaning of the base word is similar to a meaning that would make sense for the word.

4. Add the meaning(s) of the prefix and/or suffix and predict the meaning of the word.

5. See if your meaning makes sense. Use a dictionary if you need to.

Read "The Birth and Death of Stars." Look for Greek and Latin roots to help you figure out the meanings of words. You may also use a dictionary to help you figure out the meanings of the Words to Know.

Words to Write Reread "The Birth and Death of Stars." Use what you know about astronomy to write a story set in outer space. Include words from the Words to Know list.

182

The Birth and Death of Stars

For thousands of years, astronomers have gazed up into space and wondered. We are beginning to understand our galaxy, the huge cluster of stars in our corner of the universe. How do we think our sun and the planets of our solar system came to be?

One idea says that they formed from an enormous spinning cloud of gas and dust. The spinning pulled most of the matter in the cloud toward the center. However, smaller whirlpools also formed in the cloud. Some matter also collected in the whirlpools. The dust particles grew closer together and began to collide with each other. As they were pressed together, the balls of matter became more compact. The matter in the center formed the sun. The matter in the whirlpools formed the planets.

The sun, at the heart of our solar system, is a star. All stars have a life cycle of many billions of years. Some stars end as a cold piece of matter—a sort of space junk. Others may explode and then collapse into a black hole. We will not get to see how our sun dies. That ending is billions of years away.

Your Turn!

 Need a Review? For more help with Greek and Latin roots or base words, see pages 176–177.

▶ **Ready to Try It?** As you read other text, use what you learned about Greek and Latin roots to help you understand it.

artifacts

decrees

receded

abundant

eternity

immortal

reigned

Vocabulary Strategy for

🎯 Greek and Latin Roots

Word Structure Many words in English are derived from Greek and Latin roots. If you recognize and know the meaning of a root in a word, you can probably figure out the word's meaning. For example, *mort* is a Latin root meaning "death." (A *mortal* wound is a deadly one.) And *reg* or *rex* means "king." (*Tyrannosaurus rex* was king of the dinosaurs.)

When you come across a word that is unfamiliar to you, follow these steps.

1. Look at the unfamiliar word. Examine the word to see you if recognize a Latin or Greek root in it.

2. Ask yourself how the meaning of the Latin or Greek root influences the meaning of the word.

3. Review the context in which the word is used. Does this meaning make sense?

4. If not, read on for other clues.

As you read "The Pharaohs of Egypt," look for Greek or Latin roots to help you determine the meanings of words. If you still can't find the meaning, use a dictionary.

Words to Write Reread "The Pharaohs of Egypt." Study the pictures on these two pages and choose one to write about. Use as many words from the Words to Know list as you can to describe the meaning of your picture.

Wilderness Camp

I woke early to unfamiliar sounds. Slowly it registered in my mind that I was not at home but in a tent in the north woods of Michigan. My whole body had stiffened from sleeping with only a sleeping bag between me and the remarkably hard ground. Why had I signed on for Wilderness Camp? I wasn't sure I could take a month of roughing it.

Soon everyone was up and concentrating on breakfast. First we would have to build a fire. We had sat up late last night until the campfire was only ash and embers that smoldered. Our counselor, Daniel, had doused it well with water from the river. An unattended campfire could start a forest fire, and we didn't want that.

I took a hatchet and began to cut a dead branch into firewood. Daniel built the fire, using painstaking care. He started with wadded-up newspaper and small dead twigs. We would lean the larger pieces of wood around this and then ignite the paper. As we worked, I showed Daniel the curious hollow stick I had found yesterday. He told me it was a quill from a porcupine.

Your Turn!

❚❚ Need a Review?
For additional help with base words, see page 176.

▶ Ready to Try It? As you read other text, use what you learned about base words and word endings to help you understand it.

Let's Think About...

Genre

Literature is classified into different types, or **genres.**

- All genres are considered either fiction or nonfiction.
- Texts with similar form and style often belong to the same genre.
- Knowing the genre of a reading selection can help you better understand what you read.
- Knowing about genres can help you better choose what to read when you read independently.

Ready to Try It?

Envision It! | Genre

Fiction
fable
folk tale
historical fiction
realistic fiction
science fiction
tall tale

Drama

Poetry

Informational Text
expository text
persuasive text
procedural text

Literary Nonfiction
autobiography
biography
journal
personal essay

Fiction Describes imaginary events or people

	Genre	Setting	Characters	Plot
	A **fable** is a short, imaginative story that tells a moral, or lesson.	Any; place and time may be unimportant to the story	Animals are often the main characters.	The moral, or lesson, is usually stated at the end of the story.
	A **folk tale** is a story or legend that is handed down from one generation to the next. It usually has no known author.	A folk tale usually takes place "long ago and far away."	Flat, or simple, characters; may be capable of superhuman actions; may be shown as "bad" or "good"	Conflict usually between two or more characters, or between characters and nature
	Historical fiction is a made-up story that takes place in the past.	Should be real or seem real; has specific focus on time and place in history	Like real people or based on real people; characters fit in with the historical time and place	Any; conflict sometimes about a struggle in the world at that time, or a great accomplishment
	Realistic fiction is a made-up story that could really happen, such as an adventure story. Humorous fiction tells the same kind of story with humor.	Should be real or seem real; may be specific to time	Think and act like real people	Realistic and believable

	Genre	Setting	Characters	Plot
	Science fiction is a type of fantasy that tells a story based on science or technology.	Time and place is usually imagined; often set in the future	Characters may be realistic.	Any; conflict often between characters and nature or technology, or between two characters.
	A **tall tale** is an exaggerated story that is often funny and contains superhuman characters.	Often takes place in the past, in real places	Superhuman abilities; sometimes fictional versions of people in history	Any

Drama and Poetry Tells a real or fictional story in a unique way

	Genre	Features	Organization	Includes...
	Drama tells a story meant to be acted out for an audience.	Character dialogue and stage directions tell the story; character list and setting description	Lines of dialogue and stage directions	Plays; sketches; skits; scripts for radio or television
	In **poetry**, words are arranged in lines that have a rhythm, or a beat. Poems do not always rhyme.	Lines of text that are rhythmic (have a beat); words often describe images or emotions; figurative language	Any; may be in groups of lines called stanzas, or in another pattern	Free verse poems; ballads; humorous rhyming poems; sonnets; shape poems; lyrical poems; narrative poems

Informational Text Provides facts, details, and explanations

	Genre	Features	Organization	Includes...
	Expository text gives facts and details about people, places, things or events.	Facts and details about real places or events; usually includes maps, photos, headings, fact boxes, time lines, or illustrations with captions	Can be chronological, build from simple to more challenging information, or use another logical order	Cause-and-effect, compare-and-contrast, problem-solution, or proposition-support essays; factual magazine or textbook articles; some speeches; articles about culture or history
	A **persuasive text** tries to convince readers to think or do something.	Tells the author's point of view; may use photos, illustrations, and persuasive words such as *must* and *should*	Often written with a cause-and-effect or problem-solution pattern; shows author's reasoning in a logical order	Reviews; editorials; letters to the editor; advertisements; some speeches; book, movie, or product reviews
	Procedural text explains how to do something in clear, easy-to-understand steps from beginning to end.	Includes a list of any needed materials; may use maps, charts, diagrams, illustrations with captions, graphs, time lines, etc.	Usually chronological; may be numbered in order of steps	Instructions or multi-tasked directions, such as recipes or rules for a game; how-to guides

Literary Nonfiction Based on facts, real events, and real people

	Genre	Setting	Characters	Plot
	An **autobiography** is the story of a real person's life, written by that person. Autobiographical sketches focus on an important event in the writer's life.	A real place in the past, from the writer's life	Real people from real life	Any; conflict often about a great struggle or accomplishment
	A **biography** is the story of a real person's life, written by another person.	A real place in the past, from the subject's life	Real people from real life	Any; conflict often about a great struggle or accomplishment
	A **journal** is a record of a person's thoughts and experiences as they happen. Memoirs reflect on a specific time or event in the writer's past.	May be abstract; usually a time and place from the writer's life	Real people from real life	Usually organized in chronological order; events from the writer's life and perspective
	A **personal essay** is a narrative that tells about a topic from the writer's perspective, using the first-person *I*, *my*, or *our*.	Any	Any; from real life	Any; topics or events shown from the writer's perspective

Acknowledgments

Illustrations
7, 9, 11, 13, 15, 17, 19, 21, 23, 25 Valeria Cis

Photographs

Every effort has been made to secure permission and provide appropriate credit for photographic material. The publisher deeply regrets any omission and pledges to correct errors called to its attention in subsequent editions.

Unless otherwise acknowledged, all photographs are the property of Pearson Education, Inc.

Photo locators denoted as follows: Top (T), Center (C), Bottom (B), Left (L), Right (R), Background (Bkgd)

35 ©John Lawrence/Getty Images
41 AP/Wide World Photos
43 ©Rick Gayle/Corbis
55 ©imagebroker/Alamy
59 ©Robert Frerck/©Robert Frerck/Odyssey/Chicago
63 ©Natalie Fobes/Corbis
65 Getty Images
73 ©Steve Skjold/Alamy Images
75 Getty Images
81 ©Robert Harding Picture Library Ltd/Alamy Images
85 ©Gail Mooney/Corbis
91 W. Perry Conway/Corbis
99 (TL, BR) ©Roger Ressmeyer/Corbis
101 Wang Lu/©ChinaStock
111 (B) ©Ed Edahl-FEMA via CNP/CNP/Corbis, (Bkgd) Jeff Schmaltz, MODIS Rapid Response Team, GSFC/NASA
116 (B) ©Ralph A. Clevenger/Corbis, (C) ©Stockbyte/Getty Images, (T) Jupiter Images
118 (T) ©George Steinmetz/Corbis, (B) ©Jeffrey Hamilton/Getty Images, (C) ©Mawroidis Kamila/Shutterstock
120 (B) ©Alaska Stock LLC/Alamy Images, (C) ©Bates Littlehales/Getty Images, (T) ©Galen Rowell/Corbis
121 ©Lori Adamski Peek/Getty Images
122 (T) ©Alison Wright/Corbis, (B) ©philipus/Alamy, (C) Corbis
124 (C) ©canadabrian/Alamy, (T) ©John Boud/Alamy, (B) Jupiter Images
126 (B) ©Ivy Close Images/Alamy, (C) ©North Wind Picture Archives/Alamy Images, (T) Jupiter Images
127 ©Chris Lisle/Corbis
129 ©Liu Liqun/Corbis
130 (T) ©Brian Tan/Shutterstock, (C) ©PhotoAlto/Laurence Mouton/Jupiter Images, (B) Jupiter Images
132 (C) ©Creatas/SuperStock, (B) ©David McGlynn/Alamy Images, (T) ©Peter Wells/Alamy Images
133 ©Buddy Mays/Corbis
134 (B) ©Dougal Waters/Getty Images, (C) ©Martin Green/Shutterstock, (T) ©Mitch Hrdlicka/Getty Images
135 ©Reed Kaestner/Corbis/Jupiter Images
138 (T) ©Jerome Scholler/Shutterstock, (C, B) Jupiter Images
139 (B) ©Frans Lanting/Corbis, (TL) ©Mark Moffett/Minden Pictures
144 (C) ©Arco Images GmbH/Alamy Images, (T) ©Tetra Images/Getty Images, (B) ©Wilmar Photography/Alamy Images
145 Tom Nebbia/Corbis
146 (C) ©Phil Schermeister/Corbis, (T) ©Warren Morgan/Corbis, (B) Shutterstock
147 ©Tomb of Qin shi Huang Di, Xianyang, China/Bridgeman Art Library
148 (C) ©Paul Simcock/Jupiter Images, (B) ©richard mittleman/Alamy Images
150 (C) ©Holly Kuchera/Shutterstock, (B) ©Michael Boys/Corbis, (T) Jupiter Images
151 ©Michael Boys/Corbis
152 (C) ©George Doyle/Getty Images, (C) Getty Images
153 (Bkgd) ©Atlantide Phototravel/Corbis, (B) ©Purestock/SuperStock, (BR) ©Stuart Westmorland/Getty Images
154 (C) ©Chris George/Alamy Images, (B) ©Mandy Collins/Alamy Images, (T) ©Robert H. Creigh/Shutterstock
158 (T) ©George H. H. Huey/Corbis, (B) ©SuperStock, Inc./SuperStock, (C) Courtesy of Oxford University Musuem of Natural History/Gary Ombler/©DK Images

159 ©Ira Block/National Geographic Image Collection

160 (T) ©imagebroker/Alamy Images, (B) ©Roy Morsch/PhotoLibrary Group, Inc., (C) Photos to Go/Photolibrary

161 ©Lee Snider/Corbis, ©Stan Osolinski/Corbis

168 (B) ©age fotostock/SuperStock, (C) ©Ralph White/Corbis, (T) ©Sereda Nikolay Ivanovich/Shutterstock

169 (CR) ©Stephen Frink/Getty Images, (T) Frank Greenaway/Courtesy of the Weymouth Sea Life Center/©DK Images

170 (B) ©Nigel Cattlin/Alamy Images, (T) ©SB Photography/Alamy, (C) Getty Images

171 Bettmann/Corbis

172 (T) ©MediaMagnet/SuperStock, (C) ©Mireille Vautier/Alamy Images, (B) ©North Wind Picture Archives/Alamy Images, (B) ©Robert Michael/Corbis/Jupiter Images, (C) Jupiter Images

174 (T) ©Classic Image/Alamy Images

175 ©Gianni Dagli Orti/Corbis

178 (B) ©Gianni Muratore/Alamy Images, (C) ©Lisa F. Young/Alamy, (T) Peter Anderson/©DK Images

180 (T) ©Chris Howes/Wild Places Photography/Alamy Images, (C, B) Jupiter Images

181 (CR) ©Galen Rowell/Corbis, (BR) ©Warren Morgan/Corbis

182 (C) ©Eric Van Den Brulle/Getty Images, (T) ©Tony Gentile/Reuters/Corbis, (B) Jupiter Images

183 (T) ©ESA/NASA/P. Anders/Corbis, (BR) ©Roger Ressmeyer/Corbis, Charles & Josette Lenars/Corbis

184 (C) ©David Chasey/Getty Images, (B) ©David Crausby/Alamy Images, (C) ©Peter Harholdt/SuperStock

186 (C) ©Joe McDonald/Corbis, (B) ©Nick Michaluk/Alamy Images, (T) Jupiter Images

187 (T) ©Larry Lefever/Grant Heilman Photography, ©Reuters/Corbis, (BR) Getty Images